D1485395

K Boat Catastrophe: Eight Ships and Five Collisions

The full story of the 'Battle of the Isle of May'

The author is a soldier – who always wanted to be a sailor. For thirty-three years, he wrote a regular humour column under the pen name 'Sustainer' which appeared in *The British Army Review*, latterly *The Officer*, and for divers other military publications, both British and foreign. Collections of these articles have been published in three books.

This is his seventh book, but his first foray into naval history. He was inspired to write this history as he can see the Isle of May and the 'battlefield' from his home in North Berwick.

By the same author:
The Colonel's Table
Reveille & Retribution
Spit & Polish
Friend & Foe
On Laffan's Plain
The Price to Pay

This book is dedicated to the memory
of the 104 Officers and Ratings
who died in the 'Battle of the Isle of May'
on 31 January 1918

K Boat Catastrophe: Eight Ships and Five Collisions

The full story of the 'Battle of the Isle of May'

N. S. Nash

Pen & Sword
MARITIME

First published in Great Britain in 2009 by
Pen & Sword Maritime
An imprint of
Pen & Sword Books Ltd
47 Church Street
Barnsley
South Yorkshire
S70 2AS

Copyright © N. S. Nash 2009

ISBN 978 1 84415 984 0

The right of N. S. Nash to be identified as Author of this work has been
asserted by him in accordance with the Copyright, Designs and Patents
Act 1988.

A CIP catalogue record for this book is
available from the British Library

All rights reserved. No part of this book may be reproduced or
transmitted in any form or by any means, electronic or mechanical
including photocopying, recording or by any information storage and
retrieval system, without permission from the
Publisher in writing.

Typeset in 10pt Palatino by Mac Style, Beverley, East Yorkshire
Printed and bound in the UK by the MPG Books Group

Pen & Sword Books Ltd incorporates the Imprints of Pen & Sword
Aviation, Pen & Sword Maritime, Pen & Sword Military, Wharncliffe
Local History, Pen & Sword Select, Pen & Sword Military Classics, Leo
Cooper, Remember When, Seaforth Publishing and Frontline Publishing

For a complete list of Pen & Sword titles please contact
PEN & SWORD BOOKS LIMITED
47 Church Street, Barnsley, South Yorkshire, S70 2AS, England
E-mail: enquiries@pen-and-sword.co.uk
Website: www.pen-and-sword.co.uk

Contents

The Isle of May viewed from the south. *(P. and A. Macdonald/Aerographic/SNH)*
This island has steep cliffs to the west, but it slopes down to the sea on the east, facing the
North Sea. It is just over 2,000 yards long and about 500 yards wide. The first lighthouse
in Scotland was erected here in 1636, but despite this, the waters around the island are
littered with wrecks. HM Submarines *K-4* and *K-17* lie off the top right of the picture. The
island was of strategic use in both world wars. *(Scottish Natural Heritage)*

List of Illustrations

The photographs and illustrations in this book have been gathered from a number of sources, the vast majority of which are readily available on the Internet and elsewhere in the public domain. Others are acknowledged where the source can be identified. However, in some cases the source cannot be identified, and their use, while not specifically acknowledged, is, nevertheless, much appreciated. Copyright holders are invited to make contact with the publisher.

Foreword

Admiral Sir James Perowne KBE.

This excellent historical account by 'Tank' Nash is about one of the less than glorious days in the long history of the Royal Navy. It describes a chain of disasters, which were completely avoidable, that took place in January 1918 when elements of the Grand Fleet were transiting the Firth of Forth to conduct exercises in the North Sea. In the ensuing chaos five collisions took place, with the loss of two submarines and 104 officers and men. It was a national tragedy, which was kept under wraps for many years, but now the full archive files are available and the horror of that day is revealed.

To the modern reader used to boards of inquiry taking years to complete, the undue haste to cover all the evidence in five days seems unreal. The author reveals the cursory nature of the court of inquiry, the lack of probing questions and the acceptance of flimsy evidence and very sparse track charts. Incredibly, the Captain of HMS *Inflexible*, Captain Hawksley, was in no way censured for failing to stop or offer assistance after his ship was in collision with *K-22*, or even to report the incident.

Commander Leir was subject to a court martial, but that also seemed to lack depth, and the court failed to really investigate the options that were open to him. It does seem foolhardy of Leir to have reversed course and combed the track of the fast-advancing Rosyth force in the dark, in poor visibility, with reduced lights showing and three submarines following in his wake: not an advisable manoeuvre.

It is easy for us to sit in judgment of those in command, but it must be remembered that submarines had only been in service for sixteen years, that they were at the limit of the available technology, and the ship's companies were becoming professional but were inexperienced as this new arm of the service rapidly expanded. In Edwardian days, being a submariner was not considered to be gentlemanly, and this new service was known as 'The Trade'. The excellent illustrations that adorn this book show the reasons for this clearly.

The author considers, in one of the closing chapters, the distribution of blame, and the overall commander of the Rosyth force, Vice-Admiral Sir Hugh Evan-Thomas, who seemed to be blissfully unaware of what was going on astern, is found wanting.

This was an officer who had not covered himself in glory at the Battle of Jutland nearly two years earlier when he commanded the 5th Battle Squadron. He was a stickler for obedience to the precise meaning of flag hoists, and had shown little initiative – nearly losing the battle thereby. He bears some responsibility for the events that took place in the Firth of Forth ninety years ago.

Since the foundation of the submarine service in 1901, 167 boats have been lost, and at least one-third of these were by accident or collision rather than enemy action. Many accidents have done much to improve the safety of the submarines: for example, the loss of *Thetis* in 1938 led to a full review of escape apparatus, and modifications to the torpedo tubes. The Thetis clip is fitted to submarines to this day. Sadly, little was learned from the 'Battle of the Isle of May', and the embryonic service did not move forward as a result.

The Royal Navy had recognized that submarines were intrinsically very unsafe, and the commanding officers had to be extremely well trained to ensure both operational success and the safety of their boats; too many were being lost through accident rather than by enemy action. In 1917, a commanding officers' course was introduced, known as 'The Perisher', short for Periscope Course, but by January 1918 only nine officers had attended and none of them were involved in this sorry saga. The Perisher is still a prerequisite for command of a submarine today, and it has stood us well over the years.

The K class of submarines was very complicated and difficult to control. Introduced by Admiral 'Jackie' Fisher to work closely with the fleet, they were steam powered on the surface and reverted to battery drive when dived. They were not a successful class, as Appendix 1 recounts. The policy of submarines being in direct support to the fleet went into abeyance but was resurrected when the next type of steam-powered submarine entered service over forty years later. The 'hunter-killer' nuclear submarine is officially designated as a 'fleet' submarine, and when first at sea was operated closely with the fleet, using its powerful active sonar to sweep ahead of the ships. This tactic was more successful and less dangerous than with the K boats, but it also has been abandoned in favour of more distant support operations. Submarines like to operate alone and away from noise.

Finally, the only expression of regret about this catastrophic performance with substantial loss of life was by King George V, and then only in a private letter; the Admiralty stayed silent.

James Perowne

Acknowledgements

This book could not have been completed without the enthusiastic and very professional support of my two researchers, Peter Gallagher and Jeff Birch, who trawled through the National Archives in Kew. This is a storehouse of national treasures, and we should all work to ensure that it has adequate funding for the future. This book draws a great deal from the original Admiralty file, ADM 156–86. The file is held in the Archives, and it documents the court of inquiry and subsequent court martial. In the interests of authenticity I have quoted, verbatim, from the transcripts of both proceedings – warts and all.

Wikipedia, the Internet encyclopaedia, provided images and a wealth of additional information. The website of the Submarine Museum and that of the Submariners' Association were of great assistance.

I am grateful to Admiral Sir James Perowne KBE, Rear Admiral Neil Rankin CB CBE, Captain Peter Grindal CBE RN and Captain Aoife Breen Merchant Navy who read my text, and whose helpful suggestions not only strengthened the book, but eliminated my landlubber's errors on matters seafaring. Thanks also to Roger Hadaway and Lieutenant-Colonel Tom Gowans who corrected my text, to Stephen Courtney, curator of the Royal Naval Museum Photographic Collection, and finally to Iain MacKenzie of the Naval Historical Branch in the MoD who contributed matters of fact and background.

The opinions expressed and any errors made are entirely mine.

Tank Nash
North Berwick 2008

CHAPTER ONE

Setting the Scene

There was a tense atmosphere in the wardroom of HMS *Crescent*, the Flagship of Admiral Sir Cecil Burney GCMG KCB, Commander-in-Chief Scottish Coast, as she lay at her anchorage in the port of Rosyth on that 28th day of March 1918.

The court martial of a distinguished officer was in progress and the accused fretted and tugged at his tie as he waited for the Court to consider its verdict elsewhere in the ship. His haemorrhoids[1] were playing up again, probably a product of the stress over the previous two months. However, it was the next few minutes that would decide the fate and the future career of Commander Ernest William Leir DSO RN. He was, at least for the moment, the Captain of the destroyer HMS *Ithuriel* and commander of the 13th Submarine Flotilla.

On a side table *The Times* carried news of the unending carnage in Flanders, and a casualty list of officers, killed in the current German onslaught, covered several pages. A highly polished brass clock ticked in the background and a white-jacketed steward tidied up cups and saucers over by the sideboard. A portrait of the Sailor King gazed down at the accused, who, in turn, glanced nervously at his 'Friend', Capt Rafe Rowley-Conwy, the officer he had chosen to assist him in refuting the grave charge laid at his door. Rafe Rowley-Conwy had been a great support over the last two worrying months.

Leir was charged with 'Negligently or by default did...',[2] and although he was well aware of the old adage that 'Every successful naval officer has to be court martialled at least once', it gave him scant comfort. The deaths of so many good men might yet be laid at his door, and the prospect was frightening.

About forty minutes previously, Ernest Leir had left the courtroom as the Court closed to consider its verdict. The evidence against him had been presented and his rebuttal of that evidence carefully noted. He had explained himself and his actions to the Court, and had to hope that it would sympathize with the dilemma he had faced.

In accordance with long tradition, his sword lay across the table behind which his nine judges sat. He knew that if, on his return, the point of the sword was towards him then he had been found guilty and his career was in ruins. There was an element of theatre in all this that he could well have done without.

There was the sound of heavy boots, followed by a sharp knock on the wardroom door. When the door was opened, the court orderly, a three-badge petty officer, was standing in the wardroom flat. He said in studied, neutral tones, 'They are ready for you now, Sir.' Leir stood and exchanged a grimace with his Friend. Together they made their way back into the courtroom, where the President, Capt William Frith Slayter, the Captain of HMS *Neptune*, would soon pronounce on finding and, if applicable, sentence.

The so-called 'Battle of the Isle of May'[3] had taken place a few weeks earlier, on the night of 31 January 1918, and it was the events of that night that had led to the trial of Cdr Ernest Leir. Not least of the factors central to that 'battle' was the performance of the nine K-class submarines that had sailed to exercise, with the Grand Fleet, in the North Sea. Five of these submarines were under Leir's direct command. However, the origins of the battle and of the K-class submarines were deep seated, and to be found long before the outbreak of 'the war to end all wars'. This being the case, it is appropriate to look into the background.

In 1805 Trafalgar had been a high-water mark for the Royal Navy, and for decades afterwards the impact of that great victory reverberated around the world. Her ships continued to be built of wood and powered by sail.

What else?

In 1811 the School of Naval Architecture was opened in Portsmouth, but far from this establishment being the immediate instrument to ensure Britain's naval supremacy by the application of the appropriate disciplines, the graduates of this school found that neither they nor their skills were welcomed. This was because there were too many closed minds in naval circles, unwilling to recognize that the world does not stand still. It was to be fifty years before the graduates of the school became a major influence in the design and construction of ships for the Royal Navy.

However, in the early part of the nineteenth century a new technology had forced its way onto the scene, and as early as 1819, a steam-driven, small ship was built and found to be highly employable. Embracing this innovative power source, the Admiralty commissioned HMS *Comet* in 1821. *Comet* was thus the first steam ship of the Royal Navy, although it has to be said she was used merely to tow ships from harbour to catch the wind – she was no more than a tug. HMS *Lightning* soon followed, and she was the first ship to be deployed on active service when, in 1824, she was included in the fleet that sailed to Algiers.

Notwithstanding the advent of steam, mainstream ship construction in the 1830s continued to be of wood, largely under the direction of Sir Robert Seppings, 'The Constructor' (1813–32). He was one of the first to apply a scientific approach to ship design when he allied the structure of the ship more closely to the burden of its armament. He incorporated a system of diagonal bracing which improved the performance of the ships he built. This is evidenced by the final generation of 'wooden walls' being about 50% longer and with a commensurate 50% additional weight of broadside when compared to a first rate of the Nelsonian period.

The evolution from sail to steam was a lengthy and uncomfortable process for the Royal Navy in the nineteenth century, as it was a very conservative organization. To a man it was convinced of its absolute superiority, and there were none to gainsay it. It could be argued that, if you have the most powerful fleet on earth and it is acknowledged to be so by one and all – then why do anything to alter that balance? As an American might have said at the time, 'If it ain't broke don't fix it.'

The Royal Navy came to accept the benefits of steam power, but there was no consensus as to how, most efficiently, to apply that power. There were two options, and these were the paddle or the screw[4] as a means of propulsion. The matter gave rise to passionate debate in mid-century, and each system had its adherents – only a direct comparison between the two eventually resolved the issue in favour of the screw.

In many cases, however, the ambitions of ship builders and architects were not commensurate with their ability. It was truly a time for innovative, skilled men to flourish – if they could be found, perhaps from the School of Naval Architecture, and then only if they could convince the diehards in the Admiralty and Treasury of the merits of their innovation. As it happens, the Royal Navy entered a period of about fifty years of bizarre ship design – a period that lasted until well into the twentieth century.

The Crimean War (1853–6) was fought on land, although the support of the Navy was critical in maintaining the logistic tail and at the bombardments of Kola and Sebastopol in 1854. These bombardments saw the first deployment of monitors[5] by both the French and British navies for the first time. It was a foretaste of things to come when, in 1855, the French deployed three monitors at the bombardment of Kinburn at the mouth of the Dnieper. These vessels were clad in iron which proved to be highly efficacious. The seven British ships engaged in this operation were witness to the success of the French innovation.

A challenging issue was the increasing emergence of iron as a material to be used in place of wood. The French commissioned *Gloire* in 1860, which was steam driven, of wooden construction, but sheathed in iron, and at 5,630 tons with a speed of 12.5 knots a formidable vessel.

Her appearance sent shivers down the Admiralty's corporate spine, and with commendable speed HMS *Warrior* was designed, built and commissioned. She was designated an 'armoured frigate', and she was the superior of *Gloire* in every department. *Warrior* was iron hulled – a purist might argue that she was iron clad. This was a major advance: bigger at 9,180 tons, faster at 14 knots and more heavily armed (40 × 68 lb guns against 36 × 6.4-inch). Her hull was stoutly armoured with 4½ inches of iron, which was backed by two layers of teak. It is here that the semanticist would debate the relative merits of 'iron hulled' or 'iron clad' – the fact is that the wooden layer was designed to reduce the threat of iron splinters. Although *Warrior*'s advanced design incorporated ninety-two rudimentary watertight compartments and six transverse bulkheads, it was not until the launch of HMS *Bellerophon* and others of her class, starting in 1866, that watertight compartments became a fundamental element of warship design.

A Capt Raphael Semmes, who was the captain of the Confederate States Ships *Sumpter* and *Alabama*, commented on *Warrior* by saying,

> Visited the Warrior…The Warrior is a marvel of modern naval architecture and for a first experiment may be pronounced a success. She is a monstrous, impregnable floating fortress, and will work a revolution in shipbuilding. Wooden ships, as battleships, must go out of use.
>
> With this single ship I could destroy the entire Yankee fleet blockading our coast.

Warrior had made every warship in the world obsolete, and she and her sister ship *Black Prince*, briefly, oh so briefly, ruled the world.

HMS *Warrior* at rest in Portsmouth harbour, and now recognized as a national treasure. (*Richard Gallagher*)

The French had thrown down a gauntlet with the building of *Gloire*, and she was to be only the first of 108 ironclad ships whose construction was started between 1858 and 1865. Britain lagged behind, and by 1865 France had completed forty ironclad ships, eight more than Great Britain.

For generations the Royal Navy was hampered by the attitudes of some of its senior officers, many of whom were quite unable to demonstrate any degree of vision. For example, the Surveyor of the Navy pronounced in 1860, when speaking of iron ships generally,

> They must be regarded as an addition to our force as a balance to those of France, and not calculated to supersede any existing class of ship; indeed no prudent man would, at present, consider it safe to risk to ships of this novel character the naval supremacy of Great Britain.

Here was a manifestation of the 'ain't broke don't fix it' philosophy. This statement was made just before the world-shattering *Warrior* was launched. The rear admiral concerned, who had been responsible for the building of *Warrior*, but who appeared not to have much faith in his creation, resigned the following year as the arms race heated up.

In his book *Before the Ironclad*, D.K. Brown sought, quite correctly, to balance the criticism by naval historians of the Admiralty and the Royal Navy as they coped with their own, internal, 'industrial revolution'. Brown comments that,

> All too often it is forgotten that an organization such as the Admiralty is not an impersonal and homogeneous entity but consists of a number of all too human individuals, widely differing in their outlook, united only in their dedication to the cause of the Navy. To all these people the well-being of the Navy mattered and there were few in which technical differences crossed the border into very bitter personal feuds. Some of these people were both innovators and highly competent.

While iron-hulled ships were practical and being built, the Admiralty hedged its bets and opted to continue to build wooden-hulled, ironclad ships as well – a decision that might just have been influenced by the vast stock-pile of timber in ship builders' hands. It was a time of great confusion, but at least the politicians were decisive. Gladstone, then Chancellor of the Exchequer, had been willing as early as 1859 to find the funds to build armoured ships if the costs could be offset by 'savings'[6] in wooden ships. In the meantime, the stock of steam-driven wooden ships was being converted and armoured. It was a compromise, but needs must…

Financial considerations have always been a factor in national ship-building projects, and there is no doubt that the more advanced iron-hulled ship was an expensive commodity. For example, HMS *Duncan*, a steam-powered, wooden-hulled, two-deck ship completed in August 1860 (5,950 tons), cost £22 per ton.

HMS *Valiant* (6,710 tons), a steam-powered, iron-hulled and armoured ship completed in September 1868, cost £48 per ton.

The skills needed to build these two entirely different types of ship placed enormous pressure on HM Dockyards, and a change in attitudes was required at every level. It is to the credit of those concerned that the challenges posed by the enormous revolution in ship design and construction were met in full.

Edward Reed was Chief Constructor, and in 1863 he realized that guns were being produced that would fire a projectile powerful enough to pierce *Warrior's* armour. The obvious solution, that of adding more armour, came at a price, and he faced a dilemma that was as long lived as big-gun ships. The building of *Gloire* and *Warrior* started an ongoing competition between the navies of the world as they all, in turn, sought to strike the right balance between gun size, armament and speed.

By 1866, the last of the wooden ships had left the stage, and naval architects were facing a vast, new and blank canvas. They had to cope with new technologies and design for the needs of a Royal Navy that had fought only two fleet actions since Trafalgar, sixty-one years before. These two engagements were much more modest in scale. In 1816, at Algiers, an engagement was fought and won against shore batteries, and in 1827 Vice Adm Sir Edward Codrington won the Battle of Navarino, but this was against an unskilled, out-gunned and anchored opposition. For the most part the Royal Navy was engaged in the suppression of piracy and in the elimination of the slave trade along the coast of Africa. It was also employed very gainfully in 'showing the flag' as a means of demonstrating Britain's power to both friends and potential enemies alike.

By the 1860s the Royal Navy appeared to be a formidable weapon that not only ensured that 'Britannia ruled the waves' but also that on land, her empire, coloured pink on countless maps, and her trade could flourish unhindered. Despite the passage of time, the Royal Navy still exhibited some of the philosophies and systems of that earlier, golden, Nelsonian age. Officers were drawn from a limited social class, and their acceptability in the smart drawing-rooms was at least as desirable as their professional ability as a sea officer. 'Change' in any form, despite it being a changing world, was resisted, and the end product was a self-satisfied and dangerous complacency in which the Navy focused a wildly disproportionate amount of its attention on spit, polish and ceremonial, all at the expense of its core professional skills. Nevertheless, iron and steam were inexorably replacing wood and wind, whether that fitted with old values or not.

An illustration of the Navy's inflexibility is the curious manner in which retired officers continued to be promoted long after they had ceased active service and had reached old age. Until the middle of the nineteenth century there was no formal system to manage the retirement of officers of the Royal

Navy, it was merely a matter of 'custom and practice'. Later, a system of sorts evolved, and in very broad, general terms all officers not in employment received half-pay. However, half-pay lieutenants and commanders were not eligible for promotion. It was different for captains and above, who, whether employed or not, could expect to be promoted by seniority. If the officer was promoted, 'To no particular squadron', he became known as a 'Yellow admiral'. That is to say, he was not appointed to either the Blue, White or Red squadrons, and therefore most unlikely ever to be recalled to the Active List. The compensation was that he could still expect periodic seniority-based promotions, but no employment and, predictably, no increase in his retired pay.

With amendments, exceptions, special cases and other diverse complications, this extraordinary system continued until the issue of an Admiralty Order, as late as 7 October 1931, which contains the operative sentence, 'And whereas we consider that, with certain exceptions, the grant of steps in rank on or after retirement should be discontinued and that officers should retire with and retain the rank last held by them on the Active List.'

There was only one practical benefit of promotion in retirement, but this was little more than an accidental by-product. Since promotion beyond captain was based entirely on seniority, this machinery did at least serve to move older officers 'upstairs' and provide a way of reaching down beyond the aged, unwilling or the inefficient, and it produced an avenue for the promotion of talented younger men who had not reached the top of their seniority list. It was only the Grim Reaper who could remove an admiral from the Navy List, and as a breed they seemed to be very long lived.

The deficiencies of the process were recognized, and clearly there were better ways to conduct affairs, but the senior officers who had the power to effect change were loath to do so, as they were likely recipients of the increased prestige that further advancement would surely bring.

Until 1842 many of the ships of the Royal Navy were designed by serving officers, and it was a throwback to that time when, in 1862, the first sign of a new approach came. A Captain Cowper Phipps Coles RN pushed himself to the fore with his design of a new type of ship; this was to be HMS *Captain*.[7] After great public debate, much of it acrimonious, the ship was laid down in 1867, launched in 1869 and completed in 1870.

The end product was a steam-driven, iron ship carrying massive sails on the highest masts in the Navy, and a gunnery turret that revolved. The revolving turret was revolutionary new thinking, and a departure from batteries of guns mounted along the length of a ship. What is more, this new configuration of guns mounted in a revolving turret worked very well. Sadly, *Captain* was deficient elsewhere. Her beam was very narrow, and this made her inherently unstable, and as a warship *Captain* was a disaster just waiting to happen. Her designed 'freeboard' – that is to say, the distance between the surface of the sea and the ship's weather deck – was only 8 ft 6 in. This made her very vulnerable, and

Captain Cowper Coles RN. The designer of HMS *Captain*, who sailed and died in that ship.

even more so when, on completion, she was found to be 857 tons overweight. This had the effect of reducing her freeboard to a mere 6 feet. For all the obvious reasons it was not advertised that this ship could only heel with safety to about 21°, a performance far below the norm for ships of this period when 70° was expected. This was a defect for which there was no 'quick fix', and while a solution was sought, *Captain* put to sea for the third time and she foundered in September 1870.

Notwithstanding that she was a steam ship, *Captain* was, like so many others at this time, also a fully rigged sailing ship, and the sails of *Captain* were the most extensive ever fitted to an iron ship. The masts that bore this vast spread of canvas were so strong that the gale that she encountered did not carry away her sails or mast – the captured wind simply drove the ship under. Only eighteen members of her crew of 500 escaped with their lives, and Coles went down with the ship. *Captain* could perhaps have functioned as a monitor for use in coastal waters, but not as a 'blue water' ship. Her design was never replicated.

The German Navy only came into being after the Franco-Prussian War of 1870–71, and despite its youth it learned shrewdly from its mistakes. The sinking of *Grosser Kurfurst* in the English Channel off Sandgate in 1878 was the result of poor ship handling, which caused a collision with another ship in company. The vessel went down within minutes, about 300 men perished and such a rapid sinking caused the Germans to rethink the fundamental design of their ships. Thereafter, with commendable speed, the internal spaces on all German warships were configured in small compartments linked only by watertight doors that could be readily closed in an emergency. The survivability of German ships owed much to the small, albeit inconvenient, size of these compartments. At the Battle of Jutland, nearly forty years later, all the German ships shared the characteristic of small compartments, and the outcome of the battle in part reflected that design feature. The Royal Navy had already introduced compartmentalization in its ships, and *Warrior* and *Bellerophon* were early examples. However, it did not apply the principle as assiduously as the Germans, and failed to learn from the loss of *Grosser Kurfurst*. The Royal Navy eventually paid the price, but as a vestigial sign of modernity it had suspended flogging as a punishment in peacetime, some eight years earlier. Now, in 1879, flogging in wartime was also abandoned; it was, perhaps, just a small step forward.

HMS *Warrior*, that first iron-hulled warship, has long since become an icon of her age. However, the ship that had changed naval thinking back in 1861 was declared to be obsolete in May 1883. She was never employed in action, but she had been the catalyst for change. Her life-span was twenty-two years, whereas that of her predecessors, all built of wood, had been much longer, and they often held their place in the line for thirty to forty years. Despite the effect of *Warrior*, for the most part British naval architects still clung to old precepts, and this was abundantly apparent in HMS *Thunderer*.

In 1879, this ship was still equipped with muzzle-loading guns, a system that pre-dated Nelson. In January 1879, while at gunnery practice in the Sea of Marmora, one of *Thunderer*'s 12-inch, 38-ton guns exploded, killing eleven officers and ratings and wounding thirty-five. The probability is that the gun had been double-loaded with powder in error. The subsequent enquiry served to convince a doubtful Admiralty that breech-loading guns had to be introduced if Britain was not to forfeit her perceived naval supremacy. To add to *Thunderer*'s woes, in July the same year, while in Stokes Bay, her boiler exploded, killing a further forty, including the Captain. All in all *Thunderer* was not a testament to British ship design.

If the hulls of HM ships were generally satisfactory, the efficiency of their guns was not. In those days, in essence, a ship was a mobile gun platform, and the guns were the be-all and end-all. Gunnery officers were considered to be something of an élite group, but regrettably the quality of gunnery in the Navy was appallingly incompetent. As an illustration of that, at the bombardment of Alexandria in 1882, it is reported that eight British battleships fired 3,000 heavy shells and managed to put only ten onto the stationary target.

Any subsequent improvements to this fundamental skill in the Royal Navy are owed, in the main, to Vice Adm Sir Percy Scott,[8] who had been present at this gunnery debâcle. He laboured mightily to put gunnery at the top of the priority list and to downgrade the importance of a ship's appearance, making himself highly unpopular in the process. He was not the only officer to express discontent with the status quo, but his was the loudest voice. He was appointed as first lieutenant in HMS *Duke of Edinburgh* in 1886, which, at that time, was the most up-to-date turreted ship in the Navy. Scott found to his dismay that gunnery was a long way down the list of priorities, and he recorded,

So we gave up instruction in gunnery, spent money on enamel paint, burnished up every bit of steel and soon got the reputation of being a very smart ship. She certainly was very nice in appearance. The nuts and bolts on the aft deck were gilded, the magazine keys were electro-plated and statues of Mercury surmounted the revolver racks. In short nothing was left undone to ensure a good inspection. In those days it was customary for a Commander to spend half his pay, or more, in buying paint to adorn HM ships, and it was the only road to promotion. A ship had to look pretty; prettiness was necessary to promotion and as the Admiralty did not supply sufficient paint or cleaning material for keeping the ship up to the required standard, the officers had to find the money for buying the required housemaiding material. The prettiest ship I have ever seen was HMS *Alexandria*. I was informed that £2,000 had been spent by the officers on her decoration. In these circumstances it was no wonder that the guns were not fired if it could be avoided, for the powder then used had a most deleterious effect upon the paintwork. One Commander who had his whole ship enamelled told me that it cost him £100 to repaint her after target practice.

Scott was a firebrand, and he steered a very dangerous course, frequently clashing with his superiors over what he considered to be their ill-judged priorities. It made him a well-known and popular character, and even led to his being immortalized in the following parody.

A Terrible Creed
(With acknowledgement to Capt Vernon Howland RCN)

I believe in Percy Scott, Captain ubiquitous, Lord of Humility, Maker of gun-
carriages,
And of all things advertised and not advertised
And in the Terribles, the heroes unlimited, the breakers of records,
And in one Dotter, invention of one Captain, the only begotten son of modesty,
by whom most things are puffed;
Who, for the Navy and our salvation, came down from Whale Island and was
self-incarnated reformer of evils,
And was made Captain, and was persecuted under the Admiralty.
Captain of the *Scylla*, Captain of the *Terrible*, Percy Scott of Percy Scott, born
not made, being one with himself and forever with the Daily Mail.
Saviour of Ladysmith, he suffered at Durban and was insufficiently rewarded.
And the next time he arose in China to slay Boxers according to the papers;
And in the fourth year he returned to Portsmouth,
And he ascended unto Balmoral and sitteth on the right hand of the King;
And he shall be heard of again, with glory belated, to teach self-depreciation
to a nation whose adulation shall have no end.
And I believe in the Deflection-Teacher, the Lord and Giver of Points, who
proceedeth from the *Scylla* and the *Terrible*, who with the Terribles together
is feted and glorified, who spake by the newspapers;
And I believe in one Loading-Tray, the key for Selection;
I confess to one Flashing-Lamp, electro-mechanical, light of lights, very flash
of very flash;
I acknowledge one Shutter for the emission of Signs,
And I look for the paying-off of the *Terrible* and the distribution of more
honours to come.

Amen.

This then was the dreadful but generally unknown state of affairs. In the 1880s
Britain's Navy could afford to look smart and well painted, for it was rarely
ever required to fight. Its presence alone was sufficient to quell potential foes; it
was all a complete myth, and very fortunately the Royal Navy's bluff was never
called. There was an urgent and crying need for a new, dynamic leadership and
for a rapid reassessment of the priorities in a modern navy. The Navy Estimates
in 1882 were £12 million, but it was going to take a great deal more money to
right the evident fundamental deficiencies in the fleet.
The transition from the 'wooden walls of England' to iron ships had been
observed at first hand by Midshipman J.A. Fisher RN, who was born in 1841.
This young man was to be the most influential individual in the Royal Navy for

Vice-Admiral Sir Percy Scott, the 'Father of Naval Gunnery' c.1916.

the better part of sixty years. He served in the Crimean War and rose swiftly through the ranks. He was present, like Percy Scott, at the inept bombardment of Alexandria; in his case, it was in his capacity as the Captain of HMS *Inflexible*.

Fisher specialized in gunnery, and his service in HMS *Warrior*, that first iron, steam-driven (although fully rigged with sails),[9] armoured frigate had given him a taste for the Navy of the future. However, as Captain of HMS *Inflexible*, he was able to gauge the painfully slow transition at first hand not least because, in 1882, his ship still retained its muzzle-loading guns. Fisher realized that as an instrument of war *Inflexible* was, at best, severely limited, and the command of this ship was an experience that helped him to develop a powerful vision for the future.

Fisher was not 'a nice chap' in the conventional sense. He was a dynamic, tenacious, pugnacious, argumentative, and extrovert character with an absolutely iron determination to have his own way. He was a bully. He was also a sailor's officer and held views on discipline well ahead of his time. He was a practising democrat and he utterly eschewed the rampant snobbery that beset the Victorian Navy. Fisher was a brilliant innovator and a dedicated officer. He was a mass of contradictions and his capacity to be charming when it suited him is not the least of these contradictions. Fisher had one overriding deficiency: he believed, without equivocation, that he had a monopoly on wisdom.

He did not.

The men who would provide the Royal Navy with its middle-ranking officers in World War I, and whose lives would be shaped by Fisher, were born in the 1880s. They were all contemporaries in the Cadet Training Ship, HMS *Britannia*, located on the River Dart, at Dartmouth. There they were accommodated in the old floating wooden hulks – symbols of what the Navy had once been[10] and a manifestation of the urgent need for modernization.

In the 1890s the Royal Navy offered a young man from the right social background a career and a profession. Entry to HMS *Britannia* was competitive, and acceptance at the college was only the first hurdle a boy had to surmount if he was to become a regular naval officer. Among the group who were born in the 1880s and who served in *Britannia* in the middle and late 1890s was Ernest Leir. He was one of those who in due course carried the burden of commanding, at least numerically, much of Britain's fleet. At the outbreak of war Leir and his peers were lieutenants, but he, and most of the others, rose swiftly to lieutenant-commander, and some to commander, on the outbreak of hostilities.

While these young men were still growing up, Fisher was making a positive and innovative contribution to the Royal Navy – the value of that contribution cannot be overstated: without his energy the Navy and the country would have been particularly vulnerable in 1914. However, to put the part he played into balance, it has to be said that he also made some dreadful ship-building decisions. These decisions, much as they were supported at the time, can now be seen, with the benefit of 20/20 hindsight, to have had a serious impact decades later, and in particular upon Leir and several of his contemporaries.

The 'Battle of the Isle of May' can be traced back as far as Fisher's early days as a man of influence in naval affairs in the last two decades of the nineteenth century.

A personal friendship with the future King Edward VII was career enhancing, and Fisher's influence in the development of the Royal Navy started to become apparent. In 1892, and by now a vice-admiral, he became Third Sea Lord. It was in this capacity that he had direct responsibility, for the first time, for ship building and design. One of the products of his tenure was the 'torpedo boat destroyer', a vessel specifically designed (as the name suggests) to combat the threat posed by 'torpedo boats'. This was necessary because several foreign navies had readily seen that a small, fast vessel armed with torpedoes was a very cost-effective way to take on, in coastal waters, the capital ships of a major maritime power, such as Great Britain.

Fisher was thus the midwife at the birth of the 'destroyer', and the first of this type was HMS *Havock*, launched in 1893. *Havock* was a small ship of only 240 tons displacement; however, she had could make 27 knots, and was well armed for her size – certainly sufficiently well armed to satisfy her role. Initially six ships of this class were ordered from three different yards. They were *Havock* and *Hornet* from Yarrow, *Daring* and *Decoy* from John I. Thorneycroft & Company, and *Ferret* and *Lynx* from Laird, Son & Company. *Havock* was the first in a very long line of destroyers. She and many hundreds of successors over the next sixty to seventy years are a remarkable legacy of Fisher's early vision.

Havock and her immediate successors were designed with the distinctive turtleback forecastle. It was a characteristic of the class, but the feature did not survive for long and was discontinued well before World War One.

It was at much the same time that, in 1893,[11] the country was rocked by the devastating news that HMS *Camperdown*, one of the Mediterranean fleet's major ships, had rammed and sunk the flagship of Vice Adm Sir George Tryon KCB. This was HMS *Victoria*, the newest, but probably one of the worst-designed ships ever to join the fleet. The peacetime disaster happened in daylight, in flat calm seas, and was unquestionably the direct responsibility of the admiral.[12]

HMS *Arab*, built in 1901 and pictured in 1904. She was one of the first torpedo boat destroyers and a later variant of the original Havock class. This was an entirely new type of warship, armed with one 12-pdr gun, three 6-pdr guns and three torpedo tubes. The small proportions of the vessel can be judged from the visible crew members. The complement was forty-six officers and men. (RN Museum)

His ship, HMS *Victoria*, sank inside ten minutes, and 357 officers and men died. The design of *Victoria* was clearly an issue, and it was concluded that her large compartments had hastened her swift demise.

Another factor was that even new ships like *Camperdown* were still being built with a ram incorporated in their bows, the ram being much favoured by the Royal Navy as a principal weapon. The rationale for this was that a ram was more likely to penetrate the armoured sides of a ship than naval artillery. This was despite the firm conclusions reached by Edward Reed back in 1861. The ram had never been used in action by the Royal Navy by this time, and, indeed, it was never to be used.

The Battle of Lissa fought in 1866 between the Austro-Hungarians and the Italians had been the last time the ram had been employed effectively, and a by-product of that battle was to extend the life of the ram in the navies of the world. A ram was an inexpensive measure to incorporate into a ship. However, it was at the expense of further technological advance in naval gunnery. The ram was a 'technology' dating back to well before the birth of Christ, and it had worked then, just as it did in the extraordinary *Camperdown/Victoria*, 'blue on blue', episode.

In 1899 Fisher was appointed Commander-in-Chief Mediterranean, and in the next three years he was able to put his mark on this major element of the Royal Navy, as well as preparing himself for the more senior appointments that would surely soon follow. He came back to Britain in 1902 and took up the appointment of Second Sea Lord, just as the emerging technology associated with submarine warfare had started to be implemented, and the first submarines were being built.

Fisher then moved, in 1903, to be Commander-in-Chief Portsmouth for a little less than two years. There was an element of inevitability when he was appointed First Sea Lord and professional head of the Royal Navy in October 1904[13] – a job he was to hold for six years. Promotion to Admiral of the Fleet followed in 1905.

In 1904, gunnery expert Admiral Sir Percy Scott, Fisher's near-contemporary, was starting to have some success in raising gunnery standards. Scott was now sufficiently senior to refuse to accept the gunsights in HMS *Centurion*. This created a furore throughout the Navy, but Fisher supported Scott's judgment, which was subsequently found to be correct, with far-reaching political and financial implications. In effect, it meant that the gunsights throughout the fleet were inefficient. In 1905 Scott and Rear Adm Sir John Jellicoe combined to effect improvements in naval gunnery, and it was in 1905 that, for the first time, the Navy achieved more hits (1,107) than misses in gunnery practice – 1906 was even better (3,405), but even then the results were unsatisfactory – at point-blank range many ships could still not land a blow on a target, and this was a target that was not shooting back! To give a broader picture, in the ten years from 1898 the average of missed shots fell from 69% to 21%. Things were getting better.

It was now that Sir John (always known as Jackie) Fisher became involved, indirectly, in the 'Battle of the Isle of May'. Fisher embarked on a massive rejuvenation of the fleet, and in the face of spirited opposition he disposed of ninety obsolete and ineffective ships and put almost as many into 'Reserve'. He correctly described the total of 154 ships as 'too weak to fight and too slow to run away'. The effect of his decision was to expose, in part, the myth that the Royal Navy had been perpetuating, because the active size of the fleet shrank dramatically almost overnight. Fisher had nailed his colours firmly to the mast. He then went further, saying they represented 'a miser's hoard of useless junk'. Well, at least everyone knew where Fisher was coming from. He reorganized the structure of British naval power and broke bones, lots of them, in the process. His name was a watchword for ruthlessness, and he slew herds of sacred cows in the interests of a stronger Britain.

There are those who believe that Jackie Fisher ranks only just below Nelson in the quality of his service to the nation. Certainly he had all the energy, single-mindedness and power so to be. None would ever doubt his unqualified devotion to his service and the nation. He was an unashamed patriot. Many of his concepts were inspired, but with the 20/20 hindsight that a hundred years bring, it can now be seen that in some cases his vision was seriously flawed. One such case was the K-class submarines, boats that had a part to play in the events that this book chronicles.

It was in 1906 that Admiral of the Fleet Sir John Fisher was responsible for the launch of HMS *Dreadnought*. This was an entirely new class of battleship; it took the naval world by storm and served to make all of the rest of the world's navies obsolete. It had the same shattering effect as *Warrior* had had nearly fifty years before. *Dreadnought* was in a league of her own and sufficiently so to set a new yardstick against which all future ships would be judged. The success of *Dreadnought* was a significant factor in establishing the respect, bordering reverence, that was accorded to Fisher at the time. However, 1906 was probably the pinnacle of Fisher's career, and thereafter he was directly responsible for some of the most expensive and calamitous decisions in British ship-building history. With the benefit of hindsight, Fisher has been reassessed, and opinion as to his merit is divided.

Fisher now had a vision of a new class of ship that was expected to combine the firepower of a battleship with the speed and agility of a cruiser. It was to be the 'battlecruiser', and in building these ships Fisher foolishly and wantonly ignored the fundamentals. A naval vessel of any size has to combine three principal ingredients: these are speed, protection and firepower. Any one of these elements that is enhanced will be at the expense of one or both of the other two. In 1861 it had been *Gloire* and *Warrior* that had been the first manifestation of this issue. The first of this new class, now officially termed battlecruiser, was HMS *Invincible*.

Indomitable and *Inflexible* quickly followed her down the slip. We will hear more of *Inflexible* later, but she and her sister ships were 8,200 tons heavier and five knots faster than *Roon*, the pride of the German fleet. The three *Invincible-*class ships all carried 12-inch guns and were very fast – 27 knots. This is on the quick side of rapid, but they were poorly protected, and in order to get those 27 knots Fisher had reduced their armour to a mere 4 inches at the bow and an inadequate 6 inches elsewhere. They were fine-looking ships but they did not win universal acclaim.

In 1908 the Admiralty found itself embroiled in the Archer-Shee case,[14] in which the heavy-handed, incompetent and weak performance of the Captain of Osborne, the preparatory school for HMS *Britannia*, exposed the Navy to ridicule and unnecessary publicity. The captain in question was Arthur Christian, and his attitudes were not untypical of his peer group – many of whom rose to flag rank in the world war that would follow.

In 1908 the Archer-Shee case attracted public attention, but there were more important issues to hand, and Brassey commented on the *Invincible* class of ships as follows,

> Vessels of this enormous size and cost are unsuitable for many of the duties of cruisers, but an even stronger objection to the repetition of the type is that an admiral having '*Invincibles*' in his fleet will be certain to put them in the line of battle, where their comparatively light protection will be a disadvantage and their high speed of no value.

These were prophetic words: the impulsive Beatty, at the Battle of Jutland, sought to use his poorly trained battlecruisers as fast battleships – and he got a bloody nose in the process.

The design of these battlecruiser ships was flawed elsewhere. Not least there was the problem of the juxtaposition of foremasts and gunnery control tops in which funnel gases were vented at 550°C. It was a similar case in battleships, but it was not a problem easily resolved. The mast that provided housing for the gunnery observer was placed abaft a funnel. This funnel exuded carbon monoxide and very hot, black smoke on a continuous basis, much to the discomfort and indeed the safety of the gunnery officer observer. The position of this officer was untenable, and his efficiency was severely impaired by this arrangement, nor did it do anything to enhance gunnery performance. The root cause of these difficulties was 'upper deck layout' – there were too many elements with conflicting requirements to fit into too small a space. This difficulty was further compounded by the rapidity with which new classes of ship were being laid down, and this prevented the lessons learned from experience with one class being incorporated into the design of its successor.

There were extensive trials on director firing from 1907 until 1912. A workable and reliable system had to be developed before a fitting programme could be started. These were early days, and the matter of co-ordinated, effective fire control at sea was, and is, a complex business. Given the tools available a hundred years ago, it is remarkable what was achieved. The machinery eventually developed for keeping massive multi-gun turrets on continuous aim was very sophisticated by the standards of the day.

Once a system had been designed and proved, then the rate of installation in HM ships was dictated by the capacity of British industry to construct the equipment.

Fisher stood down as First Sea Lord in 1910, aged 70. He had achieved a great deal, and had transformed the Royal Navy into a modern fighting force. It was now in generally much better order than it was when Fisher came to the Admiralty. Notwithstanding his retirement, the old admiral still wielded enormous influence behind the scenes, and he continued to do so until his death.

It must be remembered that up until the end of the twentieth century field marshals[15] and admirals of the fleet did not retire. Although Fisher may not have been in an active appointment, he retained the right to express an opinion, and he expected that opinion to be respected. This influence was exercised discreetly and in private.

Today it is much changed, and the influence of very senior officers is vastly reduced. The military establishment has slipped down the political food chain, and for the most part the only solace for senior officers, no matter how distinguished, is to write despairing letters to *The Times*, in which they can comment adversely on the system that they once helped to manage. These officers have little or no influence on national politics or on public life generally. Once they retire they are limited to offering advice to their successors in uniform.

Membership of the House of Lords is bestowed on a very few privileged servicemen, and usually they make only a modest and unheralded contribution to the defence of the realm from that place. However, the House does provide a forum, and it was significant and highly unusual, unique perhaps, when as recently as November 2007, six former Chiefs of the Defence Staff (all members of the House of Lords) attacked HMG publicly and vehemently for its neglect of the armed forces. This was by any standards an exceptional situation, and it was triggered by the pressure of fighting wars on two fronts.

Back in 1911, and then only because of the implacable Sir John Jellicoe (by now a renowned 'nit-picker'), director firing was installed in HMS *Neptune*. She was the first to be so equipped with a system that provided centralized control of all of a ship's main armament. The general rule was that a ship should always aim to bring all of its main armament to bear on a target, which ideally was 'end-on', and this is what Jellicoe did at Jutland. In naval parlance he had 'crossed the T'. However, the modernization of HMS *Neptune* was not an immediate panacea, because 'one swallow does not make a summer', and throughout all the other capital ships of the fleet, the gun control officers were still often shrouded in smoke from the funnel, although sometimes their prayers for a helpful wind were answered.

Admiral of the Fleet Sir John Fisher GCB OM GCVO, 1841–1920.

The urgent introduction of director firing throughout the fleet was clearly a priority, and when Winston Churchill became First Lord of the Admiralty in 1911 he threw his weight behind Jellicoe and Scott – as it happens, not a moment too soon.

Despite the urgent representations of Admiral Sir Percy Scott, and right up to 1912, ships continued to be built with the mast abaft the funnel. Scott again approached Winston Churchill, who acknowledged the problem of deck layout that countless admirals had wrestled with. There was a need to re-fit about twelve ships, and it was going to be an expensive business, but Churchill insisted and the changes were duly carried out.

Sir Percy Scott was clearly an exceptional man, and he has been described as 'the father of modern naval gunnery'. Certainly, the Royal Navy owes him a great deal, but at the time his sage advice was often ignored. This was perhaps because he was so obviously single minded about gunnery issues that his expertise in this one area affected his credibility in non-gunnery matters. For example, when the Admiralty constructed ships with masts insufficiently robust to bear the weight of the new gunnery director equipment, Scott said so. His advice was rejected and only acted upon later in the war, when it became evident that masts were collapsing under the weight.

The mistakes being made by the Admiralty were observed by the Germans, and with characteristic efficiency they incorporated the best feature of the *Invincible* class into their equivalent ships, but did not compromise on protection. Their wisdom was to be amply proved at Jutland just a few years later. Fisher, meanwhile, persisted in his demands for fast battlecruisers, and threw all caution to the winds. He took the view that a speedy, heavily gunned ship could strike its opponent so fast and so often and to such effect that there would be no return fire, and therefore armoured protection was not needed. Fisher's view was that speed alone was tantamount to success.

This is an incredibly naive position for a distinguished admiral to take, and given his perceived wisdom all gained during a lifetime of service it is a culpable one. Fisher did not just want speed; he wanted 30-knot ships carrying ten 16-inch guns and virtually no armour. Common sense had flown out of the scuttle, and it seemed that there was no one to curb the Admiral and thwart his ambitions. At the top of the Navy the two senior naval officers making the running were now Vice Adm Sir John Jellicoe and Vice Adm Sir David Beatty; they were not able to resist a former First Sea Lord, and made no attempt so to do.

The relationship of these officers is interesting. The career of any service officer is completely dependent upon the degree of support he can accrue from his senior officers – usually men about five to ten years his senior: that is to say, the officers who report upon his performance and potential to hold a higher rank. Jellicoe and Beatty were, to a great extent, the products of Fisher's patronage, and Beatty to a lesser extent upon Jellicoe and the reports the former wrote. Fisher was vastly the senior, followed by Jellicoe and then Beatty, but the march of events and time changed the order of influence, if not the seniority. By 1918 Beatty was the ascendant admiral, Fisher remained an *éminence grise*, but Jellicoe was a broken man.

By 1918[16] Beatty was remarking that Jellicoe was talking 'childish twaddle' and describing Fisher as 'that arch ruffian'. There is precious little gratitude in the system then or now.

Admiral Sir Arthur Knyvet Wilson VC GCB OM GCVO. Bart. The First Sea Lord, 1909–12. He was known to the sailors as "Old 'ard 'eart". He was a brave man, and he won his VC ashore during the war in the Sudan. However, he was by no means a visionary.

The submarine was a new beast in the maritime jungle of the early twentieth century, and it was treated with considerable suspicion by the British naval establishment, which was slow to grasp the world-changing potential of this new form of warfare, although, in the very early stages, it could be said that they were less submarines and more accurately 'submersibles'.

The courage of the first generation of submariners who trusted themselves to the rudimentary boats now coming down the slip is remarkable. However, a widely held view was that expressed by Admiral Sir Arthur Wilson VC (whom we can safely presume to be English born and bred). He said in trenchant tones that, 'Submarines are unfair, underhand and damned un-English.' The Admiral was not a man for sitting on the fence, and he went on, adding, 'Any submariner captured should be hanged as a pirate!' These remarks gave rise to the custom, which survives to this day, of submarines flying the 'Jolly Roger' on returning from a successful war patrol. The Jolly Roger is invariably embroidered with emblems representing their operational successes.

The tactical use of submarines, taking into account their unique characteristics, had not been thought through. When they were introduced into the Royal Navy they were viewed in much the same way as surface ships, and organized accordingly.

In June 1913, the now Lord Fisher, 1st Baron of Kilverstone, remarked to the then Vice Adm Sir John Jellicoe, 'The most fatal error imaginable would be to put steam engines in a submarine.' What prophetic words they were – but, nevertheless, that is exactly what the Admiralty did, and, what is more, it did so at Fisher's behest, and Jellicoe did not protest.

The Admiralty was urged by Fisher that it needed submarines fast enough on the surface to keep pace with the fleet, and furthermore that they were to be not only the fastest but, as a by-product, the biggest boats[17] afloat.

At about the same time the perceptive Prime Minister, A.J. Balfour, wrote to the retired, 73-year-old Fisher, to seek the Admiral's opinion on what he saw as the threat posed to Britain by enemy submarines. In June 1913 Fisher responded to Balfour's concerns, at length, and made it clear that the sole function of a submarine was to sink ships. It was, in essence, a weapon of offence and not defence. Fisher wrote that submarine warfare was a barbarous business, but 'War is violence and moderation in war is imbecility.' He added that neutral shipping was also at high risk in any war between two maritime nations. Fisher's views, which subsequent events proved to be absolutely correct, were not well received in some circles, and they generated *Angst* to the degree that the new Prime Minister, Asquith, did not permit their wider circulation.

The First Sea Lord, Prince Louis of Battenberg, who had been appointed in 1913, was just one of Fisher's most senior opponents. He was particularly incensed by Fisher's suggestion that merchant ships, and neutral ships at that, were likely future targets for submarines. He was unable to accept the utter ruthlessness of the German submarine fleet that was soon to be demonstrated. Events moved quickly in the first few weeks of the war, and Prince Louis was swept away after the Navy's early losses to submarines and the suspicion that his German birth had generated. Admiral of the Fleet Lord Fisher was recalled to active service, and he was back in harness as First Sea Lord by late 1914.[18]

Regardless of his earlier position on steam submarines, Fisher was now determined to have 'fleet' submarines, and what is more was in a position to do something about it.

The submarine, by its nature, has to operate as a singleton predator, and, notwithstanding the German wolf pack system of co-ordination during World War II, always did and still does. A number of submarines, acting in concert, in close company and operating at high speed on the surface as part of a large surface fleet, is one thing. But once submerged, they would be more of a hazard to each other and friendly surface ships than to any enemy. Nevertheless, Fisher held firm to the view that the fleet had to have 'fleet' submarines, operating in flotillas on the surface and in proximity when submerged. He saw them as an essential component of the fleet, providing the capability he demanded. Fisher's dominance as a service officer over his uniformed contemporaries, senior ministerial and civil service colleagues has never been matched before or since. His personal qualities were such that none would oppose him: that, on the one hand, made him an effective leader, but on the other it also made him, potentially, very dangerous.

Fisher's position was that with such a mix of surface and submarine vessels the fleet would have overwhelming power when matched against any likely foe. With this policy in place, eight J-class boats were built to meet Fisher's requirements. When eventually delivered they did not meet Fisher's specification as, even when flat out, they could manage only a derisory 19 knots. This was very fast indeed by the standards of the day, but patently not fast enough to keep up with a fleet moving at 21–25 knots. Fisher was not a happy admiral, and he sent his people back to their drawing boards.

This deficiency in the J boats could not be bettered by a diesel motor, and it was against that background that Vickers Ltd suggested that it had the expertise to design and build oil-fired, steam-driven boats that would provide the 24 knots desired. This was the genesis of the ill-fated K-class boats to which many gallant men entrusted their lives.

Their design attracted vigorous debate, and it was 'condemned as obsolete even before the boats were built'.[19] They were, in fact, so fast that no submarine of World War II could have matched them. Sadly, the design of the K boats was dreadful. A steam-turbine-driven vessel had to have a funnel to expel the combustion fumes of the boilers, and the K boats had two such funnels. When the boat dived the funnels were swung into housings in a horizontal position and the furnaces were 'damped down'. Similarly there were two large air intakes, one above each turbine, and they too had to be sealed. Little wonder then that those early submariners commented that the class had 'too many holes in the hull'. The imperative to ensure that the orifices in the boat's hull, such as the funnels when protruded, were watertight when the funnels were retracted for diving, needs no amplification here.

Even a damped-down furnace generates heat, and the boats must have been uncomfortably hot. That same damped-down furnace consumed oxygen and limited the endurance of the K boats when submerged.

The design of the K boats was for a craft, double-hulled, that displaced 1,883 tons on the surface and 2,570 tons when submerged. By any yardstick, these were going to be very large boats. They were to be 339 ft long with a beam of just less than 27 ft and a height of 21 ft. In addition to its oil-fired steam turbines, each boat had an auxiliary diesel generator to power the four electric motors and charge the batteries. The electric motors were essential when submerged, and with them the boat was able to achieve 9 knots. But it was the magic 24 knots on the surface that made them so very attractive to Admiral Jackie Fisher. Not only was the K boat fast but she was to be heavily armed. She had three guns – two 4-inch and one 3-inch AA gun. This latter gun was forward thinking because, although attack from the air was still only a relatively minor threat, that threat was growing with the rapid advances in aviation technology. The boat was designed to mount ten 18-inch torpedo tubes, two of which were built into the funnel structure for use in surface engagements. The complement of each K boat was to be about sixty officers and ratings.

In June 1915 contracts were placed for the first four K boats. Portsmouth Dockyard was to build *K-1* and *K-2*, and Vickers Ltd was to build *K-3* and *K-4*, at an anticipated cost of £300,000 per boat. *K-3* was the first boat to be completed, and very soon the deficiencies in the design became apparent. The K class were poor sea boats. In heavy seas and when travelling fast they shipped water in through their funnels and the water extinguished the boilers! They were designed to submerge to 200 ft, but as this was considerably less than the length of the boat, and depending on the angle of the dive, the stern would be on the surface when the bow was at the safe diving limit. The internal bulkheads were designed for a maximum depth of 70 ft, well short of the proposed submerged range. The boats were cumbersome, uncomfortable and inefficient. It is little wonder that British sailors of 1915 did not take the class to their hearts. A brief history of the K-class submarine is to be found at Appendix 1.

In 1915 Fisher, convinced of his sound judgment, was now planning the building of the biggest ship in the world. She was to be HMS *Incomparable*. And incomparable she would certainly be: 1,000 feet long with a top speed of 35 knots, she was to mount six 20-inch guns; and again, armoured protection was to be minimal. Meanwhile the battlecruisers continued to move smoothly down the slipways. *Tiger, Repulse, Renown, Indefatigable, Queen Mary, Courageous,*[20] *Furious* and *Glorious* had been launched; *Hood* would follow in due course. Eventually, the majority were to perish with enormous loss of life and without bringing distinction to their class.

Fisher resigned his office in 1915. He was at odds with the Cabinet over the conduct of operations in the Dardanelles, and despite protests from Winston Churchill the old admiral was adamant. He handed over to Admiral Sir Arthur Knyvet Wilson, who, in turn, was to be replaced by Admiral Sir John Jellicoe in December 1916. Thus the Royal Navy had had four First Sea Lords in the space of less than three years – and when Jellicoe was sacked it had had five in four years. Although now out of office, Fisher, predictably, continued his crusade from behind the scenes, and by now he must have been delusionary because he returned his attention to submarines.

He announced that he had a plan for a boat with a 12-inch gun. Amazingly, he also entertained the vision of a submarine cruiser of 30,000 tons with eight 18- or 20-inch guns.

Visionary?

Admiral Sir John Jellicoe GCB OM GCVO (1859–1935), Fisher's choice to command the Grand Fleet and who had limited success at Jutland. He was sacked as First Sea Lord in 1917 and became Governor-General of New Zealand, 1920–24.

Well perhaps. But vision has to be related, at some stage, to practicality, and quite how this particular beast was to operate remains unclear. It is probably as well that it was never built.

Although the advances made in technology, design, production, training and general manpower matters during the previous twenty years were enormous, the downside was an ample element of incompetence and flawed vision. The Navy, naval architects, weapons designers and industry were charging into the unknown, and that they got so much right is to the credit of all concerned and at every level.

After fifty years of evolution in which the Royal Navy had combined, paradoxically, innovation with ineptitude, imagination with inefficiency and progress with paralysis, it entered into World War One. The last few decades had been turbulent and expensive. The new ships were untested, as were virtually all of the senior officers who were to command these latest weapons and implement new tactical doctrine – not least in submarine warfare.

The war had started on a most inauspicious note when, in September 1914, RMS *Oceanic*, which had been taken into naval service, armed and designated for patrol work around the northern shores of Scotland, the Shetland Isles and Faeroes, ran aground on the notorious and well-charted 'Terrible Shaalds'. This reef was thirteen miles off the ship's intended track, and it claimed *Oceanic* on her first cruise under the White Ensign.

A Capt R.N.W. Slayter RN was in command, but also aboard and with an undetermined role was her former civilian master, Capt Henry Smith MN. It was an unhappy arrangement. Slayter was himself an experienced navigator and he had given specific instructions as to the general course to be steered. However, Capt Smith took charge when Slayter retired for the night, and he decided to ignore Slayter's wishes and gave the navigating officer new instructions entirely of his own making.

Slayter sensed a change in the ship's movement, returned to the bridge and to his chagrin, realized, too late, that the navigator had deviated from the correct course. He countermanded Smith's instructions and then made a hasty and ill-judged decision that led directly to the grounding.

An early picture of *K-3*, showing evidence of her motive power from both funnels. The early, low-profile bow should be compared with the much later design of *K-26* on page 131. (*Submerged Productions*)

Slayter's enviable reputation as a navigating officer[21] was damaged. Although, as the Captain, he was not also expected to function as the navigator in *Oceanic*, he was, nevertheless, 'In Command' and being 'In Command' is a non-negotiable state – you either are or you are not. In this respect someone once likened it to pregnancy. Inevitably, the ignominy of the stranding did nothing for Slayter's career.

Despite several salvage attempts, *Oceanic* could not be saved, and the 17,272-ton luxury liner and pride of the White Star Line was a total loss. Both Slayter and Smith were tried by court martial. Slayter, however, declined to accept the time-honoured moral responsibility that goes with command. He insisted, instead, that Smith share in any blame, if blame there was to be. Both captains having been tried, they were promptly exonerated.

Justice was then seen to be done when the navigator was reprimanded!

Just like the events that this book chronicles, the stranding of *Oceanic* was not publicized – indeed it was shrouded in secrecy. Hardly surprising really, because a world-famous ship, in sound mechanical order, in home waters, in calm seas and under Royal Navy command, had been firmly positioned on the top of a well-charted reef. It would have had a deleterious effect on national morale had the facts been known, and so they were suppressed. Why not, when, apparently, no one was to blame anyway?

When war was declared Germany had a total of only fifty-seven torpedoes, but within three weeks and for the expenditure of seven of these torpedoes the world had changed. The efficiency of the German submarine fleet was quickly demonstrated in early September 1914 when *U-21* torpedoed and sank HMS *Pathfinder* off St Abb's Head with the loss of 259 officers and men. *Pathfinder* thus had the dubious distinction of being the first British ship to fall victim to a torpedo.

Only days later, on 22 September, off the Dutch coast, three old heavy cruisers, *Aboukir*, *Hogue* and *Cressy*, manned by ill-trained crews, were all sunk by

U-9 using just six torpedoes. In total, 1,459 officers and men were lost. This completely avoidable debâcle was the result of deficient leadership and was a public scandal. Rear Adm Christian,[22] who was the commander of these three cruisers, was actually ashore at the time. He survived the subsequent enquiry, but the affair was to be a factor in the eventual resignation of Prince Louis of Battenberg as the professional head of the Navy.

U-9 struck again on 15 October, when she sank HMS *Hawke* off Aberdeen and 500 men went down with that ship. By now the Captain of *U-9*, *Leutnant* Otto Weddigen, had become a German national hero, and his exploits, which were widely advertised, had an impact on the Royal Navy out of all proportion to the size of his boat and the number of men under his command.[23]

The hard fact was that Weddigen had inflicted more damage on the Royal Navy than Nelson suffered at Trafalgar, and his exploits had an immediate and profound effect. It could be argued that this junior German officer had as much influence on British naval policy as any of a number of home-grown admirals.

The German submarine force became the 'bogey man' in British naval thinking, and the New Year only served to reinforce that status. Indeed, 1915 did not bring a change in fortunes because, on New Year's Day, to make things worse, HMS *Formidable* was torpedoed in the North Sea. A rumour started at about this time that the Germans had developed a submarine so fast that it could pursue surface ships, and it was alleged that that was what might have happened to *Formidable*. The naval establishment overreacted to this myth and, abandoning common sense, took the rumour at face value.

The Admiralty believed that the unsubstantiated report reinforced the case for fast fleet submarines, and, when coupled with the run of German submarine successes, Fisher's determination to equip the Royal Navy with the biggest, fastest submarines anywhere at sea seemed to be prudent. The K-class boats fitted that particular bill, and in part they were the legacy of Otto Weddigen.

The highly successful German submarine *U-9*. (*Submerged Productions*)

Not only were the German submarines efficient, they were also ruthless, a matter forced on national consciousness when RMS *Lusitania* was sunk in May 1915 with the loss of almost 1,200 civilian lives. Equally, the threat posed by these predatory, new and thoroughly 'damned un-English' weapons made it imperative that the major anchorages of the Royal Navy be protected.

Rosyth, in the Firth of Forth, although thirty miles from the sea, is approached by a very wide navigable channel, and this had to be closed to enemy ships. A series of anti-submarine booms were laid, and these incorporated, where practical, the islands in the Firth. It was a significant task as, for much of its length; the Firth is up to ten miles wide.

The booms consisted of stout cables from which were suspended heavy nets. The booms had 'gates' to allow friendly warships and merchantmen access to the North Sea. One of the principal booms stretched from the island of

Leutnant Otto Weddigen, Captain of *U-9*, wearing his Iron Cross awarded in October 1914.

Fidra[24] to the Isle of May, a distance of 11¾ miles. A further boom, just over five miles long, closed the gap between the Isle of May and Fifeness.

The Fife coast is sprinkled with a number of attractive fishing villages, and they made excellent bases for the boom defence vessels. These were small civilian craft pressed into service, lightly armed and captained usually by a junior RNR[25] officer. Among their number were HM Yacht *Shemara* and HMATs[26] *Strathella*, *North King*, *Cave*, *Good Hope* and *Culblean*. As a group their organization seems to have been curiously informal and commensurately ill disciplined. This is a reflection on the manner that these small ships were crewed – not by regular servicemen, but mostly by fishermen and small-boat seafarers conscripted for wartime service. It is no surprise that they did not conduct themselves in the manner prescribed at Whale Island. The role of these small ships, although vital for the security of the fleet, was nevertheless very tedious. Life consisted of endless patrols at the mouth of the Firth of Forth, often in inclement weather and in a small ship in which luxury was probably limited to a cup of Navy cocoa, known as 'Pusser's Ki'.

At the battles of the Dardanelles, Dogger Bank and Jutland, in various combinations and proportions, either poor ship design, inadequate communications, appalling gunnery, bad luck or inept leadership (especially by Beatty) had served to reject the victories that were there for the taking. There was no lack of courage or commitment at the junior level, and young

HMAT *Strathella*. One of many similar vessels employed for inshore work by the Royal Navy. *Strathella* was of 429 tons. She made 10 knots and was armed with one 12-pdr gun. HMAT *Culblean* was similar in appearance but slightly larger. (Conway's *All the World's Fighting Ships 1906–1921*)

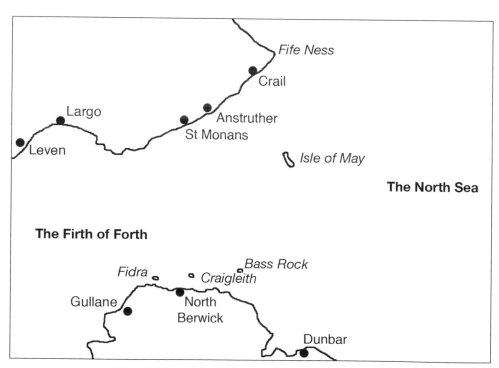

The eastern reaches of the Firth of Forth, showing the strategic importance of the Isle of May. The chosen track for the Rosyth force was to be between the island and Anstruther. This is a passage about five miles wide. Edinburgh and its port of Leith, with Rosyth on the opposite bank, are off the page to the left, about thirty miles away.

British officers and sailors acquitted themselves with distinction when given the opportunity; where there were deficiencies they were deeply rooted in the senior command and political structure. The German submarine fleet had proved to be a formidable adversary, and effective countermeasures were slow to be implemented. The cost of delay was measured in lives lost.

Post Jutland the Royal Navy had confined the German High Seas Fleet to port, and that was something of a success. However, the German fleet was still intact, and it remained an ever-present threat.

In the previous three years there had been too many avoidable mistakes, and as 1917 turned into 1918 it was becoming painfully clear that, so far, World War I had not greatly enhanced the reputation of the Royal Navy.

Notes

1. The service record of Cdr Leir.
2. ADM 156–86.The record of the proceeding of the court martial of Cdr Leir.
3. The island is described variously as 'May Island' or 'the Isle of May'. Throughout this book the latter name is used.
4. In 1845 HMS *Rattler* and HMS *Alecto*, both vessels of about 800 tons, competed to test the two systems. *Rattler* was powered by screw and *Alecto* by paddle. Over an eighty-mile trial in calm weather *Rattler* was the faster by 23 minutes. Against a headwind and over a sixty-mile course the margin of 40 minutes was more pronounced and conclusive in favour of *Rattler*. In a final test *Rattler* and *Alecto* pulled against each other. *Rattler* pulled her opponent astern at 2½ knots. The paddle-powered warship was consigned to history.
5. A barge with low freeboard designed to act as a gun platform with very limited capacity for manoeuvre.
6. This search for 'savings' continues to this day. For service in the second decade of the twenty-first century the MoD has contracted to build two very large aircraft carriers. However, this was only agreed when the Navy accepted major reductions in the frigate fleet.
7. Coles was a successful naval officer and described as 'brilliant and arrogant'. He had a flair for PR, and his campaign for the building of *Captain*, in the face of reasoned objections from Edward Reed, the Chief Constructor of the Navy, was very skilful and tenacious – and ultimately successful – although his project took eight years to bear fruit.
8. Born in 1853. Midshipman in 1866. Captain of HMS *Scylla* 1896. Died in 1924.
9. This was the origin of the unusual order, 'Down funnel, up screw'.
10. The Royal Naval College in its present form was not built until 1905.
11. The Naval estimates for 1893 were £15M and manpower 80,000.
12. Also culpable were the Admiral's subordinates who did not have the courage to challenge an order that was patently dangerous. The future Admiral of the Fleet Lord Jellicoe was a survivor of this accident.
13. The Naval Estimates for 1904 were £38 million and manpower 150,000.

14. This was the basis of Terence Rattigan's play, *The Winslow Boy*, a play first produced in 1946.

15. The rank of Admiral of the Fleet was first established in 1690 and was discontinued in peacetime in 1996. The last in that line of 120 was Sir Benjamin Bathhurst GCB, who was promoted in July 1995. Similarly, the ranks of Field Marshal and Marshal of the Royal Air Force have both been put in abeyance in peacetime, and they are highly unlikely ever to be revived. Although the measure was introduced as a 'saving' in a defence review, the armed forces are now so small that there is no place for five-star officers.

16. Both Jellicoe and Beatty were subsequently promoted to Admiral of the Fleet on 3 April 1919.

17. It is a curiosity of the RN that 'boat' is only applied to small craft serving a warship (as in 'ship's boats') or to submarines. To describe a 'ship' as a 'boat' is to risk giving deep offence in naval circles.

18. The Naval Estimates in 1914 were £53.5 million.

19. Submariners' Association, Barrow-in-Furness.

20. *Courageous* played a small part at the Battle of the Isle of May.

21. Capt Slayter had long experience as a navigating officer and his service record is illuminated by numerous testaments to his skill and accuracy. One report simply says, 'A better (N) officer is nowhere to be found'. A little over three years later Capt Slayter would have an important part to play in the story of the Battle of the Isle of May.

22. This was the same officer who, as Captain of Osborne, in 1908, conducted the investigation into the case of Cadet Archer-Shee. He initiated a serious miscarriage of justice that became a national issue. Christian emerged with scant honour and little credit. The affair had no effect upon his career, nor did the loss of his three ships.

23. He was killed in 1915 when HMS *Dreadnought* rammed and sank *U-29*, then under his command.

24. Fidra is an island that lies off the south coast of the Firth of Forth and is said to have been the inspiration for R.L. Stephenson's *Treasure Island*. The island has a lighthouse and is south-west of the Isle of May. Fidra is, in fact, further away from the Isle of May than the islands of Craigleith, Lamb, and Bass Rock, but it was selected as the anchor point because it has the easy access that the other islands lack. A further advantage is that there is no navigable passage between Fidra and the southern coast.

25. Royal Naval Reserve.

26. HM Armed Trawler.

CHAPTER TWO

At Anchor

At the Battle of Jutland, in May 1916, and under the command of Admirals Sir John Jellicoe and Sir David Beatty, the Royal Navy had won a Pyrrhic victory. A total of fourteen British ships were sunk, with 6,094 bluejackets lost. The vaunted, lightly armoured battlecruisers ordered by Fisher were found sadly wanting. HMS *Indefatigable*, *Queen Mary* and *Invincible* were all sunk, and so were three armoured cruisers, and a total of eight destroyers and torpedo-boats. The Germans lost eleven ships, but their 'butcher's bill' was a more modest 2,551. Nevertheless, the effect of the battle was to confine German surface ships to port, and after Jutland they put all their energy behind their already well-proved submarine force.

Sir John Jellicoe in his role of Commander-in-Chief of the Grand Fleet at Jutland was famously described by Winston Churchill as 'the only man who could lose the war in an afternoon'. As it happens, he did not, and he was honoured for not doing so. However, in late 1916, Jellicoe, having been kicked upstairs to be First Sea Lord, was a man beset by demons. Not the least of these was the German policy, instigated by Tirpitz,[1] of unrestricted submarine warfare, with a force which proved to be so devastatingly effective that it

Vice-Admiral Sir Hugh Evan-Thomas with 'Jack' in 1917 on HMS *Barham*, the flagship of the 5th Battle Squadron.. He was appointed to command the Rosyth element of the Grand Fleet for Exercise EC1. *(RN Museum)*

almost brought the UK to its knees as one in four of the merchant ships leaving British ports was sunk. Curiously, the policy, despite its obvious success, was not universally supported in Germany, where the impact it was having on the USA caused justifiable concern.

Jellicoe, the First Sea Lord, responded weakly to the highly effective German submarine offensive, and it soon emerged that he was a defeatist, unable to delegate and with a penchant to deal in the detail of an issue rather than concentrating on a bigger picture. He could find no answer to the catastrophic losses being suffered from the twin weapons of torpedo and mine. Despite his superiority in surface ships, not only had he no answers but, moreover, he was implacably opposed to the employment of a convoy system. His intransigence cost the country dear. In February 1917 eighty-six ships were lost, a further 103 in March and an appalling 155 in April. Jellicoe was fortunate to cling on to his job, but he was eventually dismissed on Christmas Eve 1917 by Geddes, the new First Lord of the Admiralty.

The events that brought Cdr Leir to face court martial had started only five weeks after Christmas 1917. Adm Beatty, now the Commander-in-Chief of the Grand Fleet, had replaced Jellicoe in December 1916, and a year later he was resolved to exercise his massive force in the North Sea. To this end, he issued instructions for Exercise EC1 in January 1918. The events surrounding the early phase of Exercise EC1 and its tragic consequences are the subject of this book. Official papers on the subject were classified as 'Secret' until they were released into the public domain in 1994.

Beatty's plan was to call together the two components of his fleet, part of which was based at Scapa Flow and the other part at Rosyth in the Firth of Forth. It was his intention to exercise the combined fleet in the North Sea and hope that, perhaps, it might make contact with the German High Seas Fleet. Jutland was by now just a bitter memory, but there existed a feeling in the Royal Navy that there was unfinished business here.

On 30 January 1918 lying at the naval anchorage at Rosyth was the 13th Submarine Flotilla (13th SF) led by the Marksman-class destroyer HMS *Ithuriel*, commanded by Cdr Ernest Leir. She was a new ship of 1,655 tons, and a much larger and more powerful derivative of HMS *Havock*, that first destroyer of twenty-three years earlier. *Ithuriel* was launched as recently as March 1916, with a top speed of 34 knots, lightly armed with two 4-inch guns and four torpedo tubes; she was ideal for her role of flotilla leader. Under Leir's command were the steam-turbine-driven *K-11*, *K-17*, *K-14*, *K-12* and *K-22*.[2]

Also at anchor were three battleships of the 5th Battle Squadron (5th BS), HMS *Barham*, *Warspite* and *Valiant*. The fourth component of the squadron, HMS *Malaya*, was in refit. The battlecruiser HMS *Courageous* and Scout cruiser *Blanche* were close by, as was also the 2nd Battlecruiser Squadron (2nd BCS), consisting of HMAS *Australia*, HMS *New Zealand*, *Indomitable* and *Inflexible*.[3] In addition, there were fourteen ships of the 1st, 3rd and 4th Light Cruiser Squadrons.

The 12th Submarine Flotilla (12th SF) was led by the light cruiser HMS *Fearless* under the command of Capt Charles Little, himself a submariner, and consisted of HM Submarines *K-4*, *K-3*, *K-6* and *K-7*.

These were the main components of what was officially designated the 'Light Cruiser Force'. It was a curious name in that it included four heavy cruisers and three battleships. This Rosyth force was all under the command of Vice Adm Sir Hugh Evan-Thomas, an officer who had come to public notice after his performance in command of the 5th BS at the Battle of Jutland. His judgment was questioned by some in the post-mortem that followed the battle, when it was alleged that the tardy arrival of his squadron into the fleet action was a factor in the outcome of the battle. However, some naval historians place any blame for this matter on Beatty, who had stationed the 5th BS too far astern of the battlecruisers.

When battle was joined the 5th BS acquitted itself with distinction, and 'through skilful manoeuvring and courageous engagement Evan-Thomas's ships inflicted serious damage upon the German fleet and protected much of the rest of the British force.'[4] This was also the view of Adm Sir John Jellicoe, Commander-in-Chief of the Grand Fleet, when he commented most favourably upon Evan-Thomas. He was described as 'an efficient officer with highly deserved reputation as a ship and squadron handler'. Furthermore he was said to be 'a lovable, straightforward and unassuming man'. The Admiral was apparently also something of 'nit-picker' and very much a typical product of the Victorian Navy. On balance, he was probably an agreeable person, but history treats him now rather less kindly than Jellicoe did.

Nevertheless, in early 1918, confidence in Evan-Thomas was high, and he was to command the forty or so ships that composed the Rosyth element of Exercise EC1. The names of the ships that had a part to play are recorded here, but time has obscured the names of the host of smaller vessels, among which there were about twenty destroyers, which acted as an anti-submarine screen.

The commanding officer of *K-4* was one of the bright young men of the Royal Navy's submarine branch. Cdr[5] David de Beauvoir Stocks DSO, *Chevalier, Légion d'honneur*, was aged 34. Despite his glowing reputation,

Admiral Sir David Beatty, Commander-in-Chief, the Grand Fleet, 1916. Appointed a flag officer at the age of 39, he was the youngest since Nelson. (*Great War primary document archive*)

only two months before, in November 1917, while on patrol off the Danish coast in company with other K boats, *K-4* had rammed her sister boat *K-1*. The latter was so badly damaged that, when her recovery proved sufficiently slow as to present a serious danger to all concerned in the rescue, a decision was taken to abandon *K-1*. She was then sunk by gunfire from HMS *Blonde*, the flotilla leader.

The loss of *K-1* did not have any discernible impact on Stocks's professional standing. His boat, *K-4*, was swiftly repaired, and now he busied himself preparing her for sea. His father was a military man, and John and Elizabeth Stocks lived quietly in Sutton, Surrey. In 1918 travel around the UK was rather more daunting than it is ninety years later, and so they did not see as much of their daughter-in-law, Cheridah, as they would have liked. She maintained a family home for David at Westcombe, Evercreech, in Somerset.

It is a matter of public record that Stocks was deemed to be a star in the making, and one of his commanders commented that he was an 'above-average, gallant, cool and most capable officer [who] has done extremely well with his submarine in the Marmara. [He is] always ready and confident in any undertaking.' Although there is no firm evidence to support any assertion that his crew also held him in similar regard, it would be unlikely that he would have won his enviable reputation without the whole-hearted support of those who served under him.

The recently appointed first lieutenant of *K-4* was Lt Cdr A.A.L. Fenner. Just a few weeks before, in December 1917, he had been granted permission to wear the Order of St Stanislaus[6] (2nd class with swords) for services in command of HMS *E-1*. Fenner was an officer held in high regard, and had been described as far back as 1913 as 'the best submarine CO I have yet served with as regards successful attacks and hits'. This was praise indeed, and in January 1918, just

K-4 was a boat that by 1918 had had an eventful career. The photograph above shows her high and very dry after an earlier incident. *(Submariners' Association)*

before he sailed off on Exercise EC1, he was further assessed as a 'capable seaman worthy of command. Handles men well.'

On 15 January he was posted, or, in naval language, 'appointed', to *K-6*, commanded by Cdr Geoffrey Layton, presumably in order to familiarize himself with a K boat prior to taking command of one of the class. He was happy about that because, although Layton was a contemporary, there was no doubt that he was a man headed for greater things. Then, at a day's notice, Fenner was moved from *K-6* to be first lieutenant of *K-4* with the redoubtable David Stocks, also a contemporary and a friend. The group of middle-ranking officers in the submarine service who filled command appointments in the 12th and 13th SFs knew each other well. Commanders Leir, de Burgh, Harbottle, Layton, Stocks, Hearn, Shove and Fenner were contemporaries, born in the mid-1880s, colleagues in HMS *Britannia* and by now comrades-in-arms and friends of long standing.

For Lt Cdr Athelstan Alfred Lennox Fenner, serving under David Stocks was about as good as it gets. He dropped just a quick line to his parents, Dr and Mrs Robert Fenner, who lived at 38 Portland Place, London, to tell them of his change of appointment, albeit wartime censorship required him to be guarded in his message. He busied himself with getting the boat ready for the exercise ahead.

In *K-4* Able Seaman (AB) Albert Spice, aged 27, worked alongside AB John Spice. The men were almost certainly cousins, as Albert's home was with his parents in Wimbledon, London, and John, at 36 the elder, lived with his parents in Merton, not much more than three miles away.

Albert's service record shows that he had been awarded the Africa General Service Medal (Somaliland Clasp) and Naval General Service Medal (Persian Gulf). Serving in the greatest navy in the world, he had got around a bit, but hitherto in surface ships. It is conjecture, but it was probably a comfort to both sets of parents that the boys were serving together, and in one of the Navy's newest submarines at that.

Electrical Artificer Ralph Hill was a regular sailor, and this new boat with its state-of-the-art electrical systems set him interesting challenges on a daily basis. Broadly, Hill was content with his lot. Ralph Hill was the oldest man in *K-4*, and at 41 was old enough

Commander G. Layton, Captain of *K-6*, as a lieutenant-commander in about 1915.

to be the father of AB William Dangerfield, aged 20, who was the youngest. Dangerfield was born just a few months after AB Thomas Young, who was 21. Young was a native of Portsmouth; his father was a prison officer serving at Dartmoor and the family home was, for the time being, at No. 1 Prison Quarters, Bodmin – what a truly unprepossessing address.

K-17 was a new boat launched less than a year before, and one of seventeen of her class. She was an unusual craft and, just like the rest of her class, something of a naval aberration. This did not concern 19-year-old Midshipman Ernest Cunningham of the Royal Australian Navy, who was excited about putting to sea the following day. This was what he had joined the Navy for. He already had nearly five years' service, having joined *Britannia*, the Royal Naval College, back in 1913. He was a career officer and he knew that careers were made at sea – not pushing 'bumph' in a naval barracks.

As the 'Mid', Cunningham was the junior officer in *K-17* and the youngest man aboard, but he had the respect of the lower deck because everyone knew that, the previous year, he had won at his weight in the fleet boxing championships. This was an achievement that transcended rank. Cunningham was a long way from his home in Hurstville, NSW; he missed his parents but was doing what his generation of young men was doing throughout the Empire, and he enjoyed his life in the Royal Navy. He was grateful that he was not in the Army, where his contemporaries were being slaughtered on a daily basis. Gallipoli was a name newly engraved on the hearts of all Australians.

Lt Cdr Henry John Hearn, the Captain of *K-17*, was no greybeard, but aged 32; he kept a fatherly eye on his young charge because he remembered only too clearly his time as a midshipman. Hearn was not a high flyer, and instead was described as 'steady and reliable'.[7] He was, nevertheless, a competent and experienced submarine commander.

The First Lieutenant of *K-17* was Lt Gerald Jackson. He had seen the exercise order for EC1 when it was delivered to the captain, and having read it found it difficult not to be awed by the size of the combined fleet of which *K-17* and her fifty-six souls formed such a minor component.

Among the crew of *K-17*, Signalman G.T. Kimbell had been sufficiently below par with bronchitis that he had been confined to his bunk since the 27th. Four days later he was feeling a bit brighter and was grateful for the attention Lt Jackson had paid him while he was down. A submarine is a confined space with a small and tight-knit community. As the First Lieutenant passed along the boat he had regularly checked on George Kimball.

A shipmate of Kimball was Leading Seaman Albert Edward Sinfield, who was something of an enigma. Aged 25, his parents lived in East Greenwich, as did his wife Ellen, where she maintained the family home at 19 Caletock Street. Sinfield, for reasons known only to himself, chose to enlist and serve under the name of Simpson. These things happen in the services, but ninety years later one does wonder why.

In HM Submarine *K-6*, on that bleak Scottish January day, Lt Richard Sandford, known to his friends as 'Baldy', was engaged in harbour routine, but he too looked forward to the forthcoming exercise. Sandford was 27 and the seventh son of a clergyman, no less a person than the Archdeacon of Exeter. He was educated at Clifton College and had entered the Royal Navy at the age of 13. He had joined the submarine service in 1914 and was now very experienced for his age and rank. Like Midshipman Cunningham and Lt Cdr Hearn, Sanford was a regular officer and sufficiently well reported upon to anticipate a bright future in the Royal Navy. His would soon become a household name.

Lieutenant R.D. Sandford of *K-6*. (*www.dropbears.com*)

The light cruiser HMS *Fearless* was under the command of Capt C.J.C. Little. An experienced submariner with a strong extrovert personality, he was a big man and a games player of 'splendid physique and an officer who brings a good brain and much thought to bear on any problem'. He was also a man who had ample personal courage, and this had been demonstrated in April 1917, when he was awarded the RHS Bronze Medal for his gallant attempt to rescue a seaman from the ocean. Little, by the very nature of his appointment, was a somewhat remote figure to his officers and crew. Like all commanding officers,[8] in the Royal Navy he was a person who led a somewhat cloistered existence when at sea. Although, given the chance, he was always game for a party and apparently was socially very adept. Charles Little was well served by his First Lieutenant, Lt Cdr H.B. Maltby, who was a particularly skilled seaman and ship handler. They both took justifiable pride in the leadership role they played in the 12th SF.

Vice Adm Sir Hugh Evan-Thomas was in command of a formidable force, and, when it joined the twenty-six battleships, nine cruisers, four light cruisers and numerous destroyers that Beatty was bringing south from Scapa, it would combine to be the most powerful fleet on earth. Little wonder then that the Germans were loath to come out to play.

The officers and men of the Rosyth force generally eschewed the doubtful delights of both North Queensferry, a small, ill-served, waterside village, and the disciplined environment of the canteens in the naval base. If not on duty the officers were to be found in the smarter hotels in Edinburgh and many of the ratings in the less savoury establishments in the Port of Leith, just across the Forth and only a half-hour trip in a liberty boat. In those distant days there was no road bridge, and a ferry or liberty boat was the only practical means of crossing the Forth to the fleshpots of Leith. The railway bridge, a wonder of the Victorian age, did provide a means of foot passage across the Forth, but it was hazardous and forbidden, and South Queensferry, the small village on the other bank, was not worth a visit anyway.

For the 'hostilities only' officers and ratings the war at sea, now into its fourth year, had been made up of long dull days at sea blockading German ports, interspersed with equally long days berthed alongside. When the exercise order for EC1 was issued and the ships' companies were briefed, albeit in a cursory manner, few expected anything other than a routine exercise, and one almost certainly without the least prospect of bringing the German High Seas Fleet to action.

The orders of the Vice-Admiral endorsed the exercise order issued initially by Adm Beatty, and specified the disposition of the force leaving the Firth. He determined that he would head the force in the battlecruiser HMS *Courageous*, in which he would fly his flag. She was to be screened by two destroyers and would lead HMS *Ithuriel* and the 13th SF. There would then be a gap of five nautical miles. The 2nd BCS would follow in line astern, led by HMAS *Australia* with *New Zealand*, *Indomitable* and *Inflexible*. After a further gap of five nautical miles, HMS *Fearless* would follow in the track of HMS *Inflexible* leading the 12th SF. Finally, the massive battleships of 5th BS, with the Rear Admiral flying his flag in HMS *Barham*, would bring up the rear. The force, once formed, would spread over a length of about thirty miles of the Firth of Forth almost to Fidra. It was some forty miles from Rosyth to the Isle of May, standing at the gateway to the North Sea, and bearing one of the oldest lighthouses in the world.

The Firth of Forth has ample navigation lights, and these are to be found on the many islands and on either shore. The record does not show if these were

HMS *Ithuriel*. A Marksman-class destroyer, 1,655 tons. Under command of Cdr E.W. Leir, and leader of the 13th Submarine Flotilla.

illuminated or not. The probability is that they were not, and that the Rosyth force navigated by dead reckoning. Nevertheless, it was all very much standard operating procedure and required no advanced seamanship in the initial phases of the exercise. It amounted to little more than keeping station; although in misty conditions it was not always easy to follow the subdued blue light that the ship directly ahead displayed on her stern. There was minimal expectation of contact with the enemy in the closed waters of the Firth of Forth, but in the area to the east of the Isle of May there was pronounced danger from both mines and submarines. These were dangerous waters, as any number of ships had already been lost either by enemy action or by the forces of nature since hostilities began.

Adm Jellicoe had initiated the building of a series of underwater defences and anti-submarine barriers toward the mouth of the Firth. Fidra was the anchor point for one of these barriers, but the full web had not been completed until July 1917. However, in addition, there was a guard force of mine-sweeping trawlers based on the Fife fishing villages, and these small ships of 300–500 tons constantly swept the approaches. Although the Firth, west of the Isle of May, was closely guarded, once out into the grey windswept wastes of the North Sea, surface ships were at risk, and a submarine contact was very likely.

Notes

1. Admiral Alfred von Tirpitz (1849–1930) was the nearest German equivalent of Fisher. He was responsible for building the modern German Navy and a specialist in torpedo and submarine warfare.
2. Boats and ships are named in their sailing order, and not alphabetical or numerical.
3. *Inflexible* was under the command of Capt J.R.P. Hawksley, an officer once described as 'a little inclined to nervousness on the bridge'. Adm Sir David Beatty said he was 'a very hard-working, painstaking officer'. This latter observation could be interpreted as 'This officer means well'.
4. *The Times*, 4 September 1928.
5. Commander equates to lieutenant-colonel in the Army and wing commander in the RAF. It is a very senior rank for such a relatively small command, say sixty men. Submarines, generally, were commanded by more junior officers until the introduction of nuclear propulsion and very considerably more powerful boats.
6. A Polish decoration.
7. Extracted from the personal file of Lt Cdr H.J. Hearn.
8. The rank of captain in the Royal Navy can cause some confusion. A captain (in rank) is not necessarily the commanding officer of a ship. The 'captain' (by appointment) of a ship is not necessarily a captain (in rank), but he is the commanding officer. He could be a lieutenant.

Chapter Three

Under Way

The 31st January 1918 was cold, as is to be expected in that part of Scotland in the depth of winter. The unremitting westerly wind blew down the Forth, and those working on the upper deck blew on their hands as they handled wet ropes and cold steel. It had been a brutal winter so far, and it was a relief that the weather had moderated somewhat. The many ships were readied for sea, and heads of departments reported to their respective captains as the day wore on. In this northern latitude daylight lingers on until about 1630 hrs, but as the day waned ships raised steam and took up their positions in the anchorage, which bustled with activity.

The anchorage was out of range of any aircraft other than a Zeppelin and, although these new weapons had once bombed Edinburgh, they were usually still as rare as hens' teeth in this part of the world. Although it was a sobering thought that, seventeen months earlier, on 9 August 1916, HMS *B-10* had become the first British submarine to succumb to bombardment from the air.

It was at 1530 hrs, that cold January afternoon, when a British seaplane sighted a submarine five miles south-east of the Isle of May, as the island stood sentinel at the mouth of the Firth of Forth. The submarine dived immediately and was presumed to be hostile. Vice Adm Sir Hugh Evan-Thomas, the commander of the Rosyth force, reacted to the threat posed by the unidentified submarine by signalling to all of his ships that, when they sailed, the fleet was to maintain a speed of 21 knots once abeam of the Isle of May so that they would pass the area of danger at high speed.

As planned, and on time, the flagship, HMS *Courageous*, led the way. She was showing a blue stern light for the convenience of the ship immediately astern. Following in her wake was HMS *Ithuriel* and the submarines of the 13th SF, *K-11*, *K-17*, *K-14*, *K-12*, and *K-22*. A gap of five nautical miles[1] was astern of *K-22* and ahead of the 2nd BCS, which was led by HMAS *Australia* with HMS *New Zealand*, *Indomitable* and *Inflexible*.

The smoke from the funnels of the coal-fired, steam-driven ships rose above the quiet waters of the Forth and mingled with the low cloud. On the port side Fife ran all the way to the sea. This was an area best known for its golf courses and its picture-postcard fishing villages, but now the golf courses were sadly neglected as many of the green keepers had answered their country's call to arms. To starboard were the Lothians, 'The Honest Toun' of Musselburgh and the mining villages of Prestonpans, Tranent and Wallyford. North Berwick, called by some the 'Biarritz of the North', looked out to the Bass Rock and the Isle of May.

Although this armada of ships was instructed to follow the same track, it would be a mistake to suppose that they all took an identical line, and the phrase 'following in the wake' is an over-simplification. In practice each ship and, indeed, each squadron or flotilla sailed to the east along a track perhaps 300–400 yards wide. The closer the ships in any one formation were to each other, the narrower the track. However, with gaps of up to five nautical miles (or fifteen minutes) between formations, the tracks of those two formations might differ considerably. In the normal course of events this was a matter of no importance.

Vice Adm Sir Hugh Evan-Thomas in *Courageous* set a course, almost due east, that would take the force through the channel to the north of the Isle of May and thence to the open space of the North Sea, leaving Fidra, the Bass Rock and modern East Lothian about eight miles off to her starboard side.

K-4 (Stocks), having slipped her buoy at 1300 hrs, anchored in Burntisland Roads at 1425 hrs, and then spent three hours waiting for 1740 hrs, when she weighed and followed HMS *Fearless* (Little), which had allowed a five mile gap to open up astern of *Inflexible* (Hawksley). Then the cruiser led her charges of the 12th SF down to the North Sea and the planned exercise. Yet another five-mile gap developed before HMS *Barham* and her two consort battleships followed on behind *K-7* (Gravener), the last of the flotilla. The speed of the fleet increased and the engines delivered an effortless 21 knots. White water foamed under the prow of the many warships as they made good speed down the Firth of Forth.

By now the last of the light had gone and, although intermittently stars were providing dim illumination, the moon had not risen. Initially visibility had been good, and as the lookouts scanned ahead they could see the blue stern light of the ship ahead in their squadron or flotilla.

Nearer to the Isle of May the visibility had reduced, and there was now a sea mist. Aboard the 13th SF Leader, *Ithuriel*, speed was reduced to 16 knots as she passed the Fidra gap, still 8½ miles short of the Isle of May. At 1845 hrs the lookout in *Ithuriel* lost sight of *Courageous* in the mist, and Cdr Leir, her Captain, increased speed to 17 knots, and then a few minutes later to 19 knots. This had the desired effect of closing the gap between the two ships and putting them back in visual contact. At 1907 hrs, the log of *Ithuriel* records that the ship was 'Abeam May Island'.

At this juncture the 2nd BCS was fifteen minutes behind *Ithuriel*, and the 12th SF was a further seventeen minutes further back. The three vast battleships bringing up the rear were a correct fifteen minutes behind *K-7* (Gravener). The carefully pre-ordained separation of the components of the fleet might have altered slightly, but not sufficiently to cause a problem, providing, that is, that all the ships stayed on the prescribed track and in communication.

They did not.

Exercise EC1
Sailing order of the 'Light Cruiser Force' based in Rosyth and under command of Vice Adm Evan-Thomas 31st January 1918

Courageous	(Flagship of Vice Adm Evan-Thomas)		
Ithuriel	(Leir)	)	
K-11	(Calvert	)	
K-17	(Hearn)	)	13th SF
K-14	(Harbottle)	)	
K-12	(Bower)	)	
K-22	(de Burgh)	)	
↑ 5 nm			
Australia		)	
New Zealand		)	2nd BCS + destroyer screen
Indomitable		)	
Inflexible	(Hawksley)	)	
↑ 5 nm			
Fearless	(Little)	)	
K-4	(Stocks)	)	
K-3	(Shove)	)	12th SF
K-6	(Layton)	)	
K-7	(Gravener)	)	
↑ 5 nm			
Barham		)	
Warspite		)	5th BS + destroyer screen
Valiant		)	

The names of the captains of the ships involved in the events are shown in brackets. Little (*Fearless*) and Hawksley (*Inflexible*) were both captains. The other commanding officers were all either lieutenant-commanders or commanders.

HMS *Fearless*. Boadicea-class light cruiser, 3,440 tons, eight 4-inch guns, one 3-inch AA gun, four 3-pdr torpedo tubes. Leader, 12th Submarine Flotilla, under command of Capt C. Little.

The first collision, 1917 hrs

The mist presented a minor problem to *Ithuriel* and her submarines, not least to *K-14*, commanded by the recently promoted Cdr Thomas Harbottle. Harbottle was an experienced submariner who had already commanded HM Submarines *C-6*, *C-31*, *E-21* and *E-55*. However, Harbottle had had his moments. In 1910 he was admonished and warned to be 'more careful in future' after *C-31* had been in collision with the ketch *The Brothers*. Five years later, while in command of *E-21*, he was 'held to blame for carrying out a dive in deep water with an inexperienced crew in a new submarine'.

Now in command of his fifth boat, Tom Harbottle was fourth in line behind *K-11* (Calvert) and *K-17* (Hearn) and the flotilla leader, *Ithuriel*. Just after passing abeam of the Isle of May, *K-11* altered course to port to avoid two small vessels. These may have been mine-sweeping trawlers operating at the portal of the North Sea and without any knowledge of the passage of a major fleet through their operational area.

K-17, following in the wake of *K-11*, also altered course, but *K-14*, further back in the mist, did not. She took no action other than to reduce her speed. It was only when Cdr Harbottle (*K-14*) suddenly sighted, probably, the same two small craft on his starboard (right) bow that he reacted to the danger. It was at about 1914 hrs that the Captain ordered, 'Hard-a-starboard'[2] to avoid the two vessels. The submarine answered to the helm and turned to port, but at that critical moment the helm jammed, and Able Seaman Curtis, the helmsman, could do nothing about it.

This single incident was to be the catalyst for all of the events of that January night which then followed in inexorable and painful succession.

K-14 started to circle out of effective control. Cdr Harbottle said later that he ordered, 'Full speed port, slow ahead starboard', in an endeavour to check the swing to port and to get out on the port wing away from the advance of the fleet. He also ordered that all navigation lights be switched on while his engineer strove to correct the fault in the steering gear. Six minutes – six crucial minutes – later, Curtis reported that the boat was now answering to the helm and the inexplicable malfunction had corrected itself. Apart from his curious little quarter-circular peregrination no harm had yet been done, although by now *K-14* was well out of station. Harbottle, drawing upon his experience, had reacted well to an extraordinary set of circumstances.

Meanwhile *Ithuriel*, unaware of the problem and not having seen the small vessels, kept to her easterly course at 19 knots, with *K-11* (Calvert), *K-17* (Hearn) and *K-12* (Bower) following. *K-22* (de Burgh), at the rear of the flotilla and on a track well to port (left) of her predecessors, suddenly saw the port and steaming lights of a vessel (*K-14*) on the starboard bow. The Officer of the Watch (OOW), Lt Laurence Dickinson, realized that a collision was probable, but nevertheless he put his helm hard-a-starboard. The poor handling quality of the K boats was never more evident than now: the boat responded sluggishly to the helm and *K-22* collided almost bow to bow with *K-14*.

The sharp bow of *K-22* sliced into *K-14*, and the point of impact was outside the double hull. The effect of the collision was to sever the bow of *K-14* and to breach the forward mess deck. The two men in that confined space, Leading Seaman Scott and Able Seaman Bowell, were thrown off their feet by the impact. They had no time to respond to the screech of tortured steel as the bow of *K-22* crashed in upon them. The deluge of cold, grey water was overwhelming, and both men were lost within moments.

Midships, in *K-14*, Harbottle responded decisively to the emergency. Drills and routines, practised a thousand times, were put into use and all watertight doors were closed. *K-14* was badly damaged, her wireless transmitter was disabled and she was down by the head. That she would sink was a real possibility, and to ensure the survival of the boat was now Harbottle's only aim.

At that time *K-14* was steering 313° (approx. north-west) and *K-22* 80° (approx. east). *K-14*'s jammed steering had caused her to circle into the path of *K-22* and meet her almost head on 1½ miles north of the Isle of May. Meanwhile, bearing down on the two stationary submarines were the twin threats of the 2nd BCS and *Fearless* leading the 12th SF.

At 1915 hrs *K-22* made to *Ithuriel*: 'Priority. Have been in collision with submarine *K-12*;[3] both ships are flooded forward.'

It was to be twenty-five minutes before this message was in the hands of Cdr Leir, and in the meantime, *Ithuriel* and the remainder of the flotilla steamed ever further into the North Sea. In twenty-five minutes a gap of about ten miles had opened up. Meanwhile, at the site of the accident, *K-22*, although badly damaged, was able to extricate herself slowly from the dangerous embrace of *K-14*. She could manoeuvre, but only at slow speed. Having moved away from the point of the collision, *K-22* now lay with her engines stopped on her original heading.

In *K-14* it was clear that anyone in the forward mess deck was lost, and an immediate roll-call established that two men were absent, these being Scott and Bowell. Bowell's body was never recovered, and it was almost certainly swept out of the damaged submarine and thence into the North Sea. Scott's body was eventually found, and he is one of the few casualties of this night who has a marked grave, in his case in Dundee's Eastern Necropolis.

Closing on the scene was the 2nd BCS, and at 1937 hrs, according to the record, the Flag in *Australia* signalled a change of course to south 86° east.[4] The alteration of course was not, however, reported to the OOW in *Inflexible* (Hawksley), and she continued on her original track for a further six minutes. In the normal course of events this was a readily corrected error, but these were not normal events, and the limited visibility did not help.

This is a key issue, and in a letter to the author, Capt Peter Grindal CBE analysed the situation as follows. The alteration to the course of the 2nd BCS was 12°, an alteration that *Inflexible* did not make for six minutes. In this time and at the 21 knots ordered by the Vice-Admiral, *Inflexible* would have steamed about 2.1 nautical miles. By 1943 hrs *Inflexible* would have deviated from her flag officer's ordered track by about two cables, or just over 400 yards, having made due allowance for the squadron's turning circle.

K-22 was in slightly better order than *K-14*, but her bow spaces were also flooded and she was badly damaged. de Burgh, her Captain, recognizing the approaching danger presented by the oncoming ships, fired a red Very light. Seeing this, *Australia* passed safely on the port side of *K-22* at 21 knots, and *New Zealand* and *Indomitable* also passed very close, indeed close enough to rock the two stricken submarines in their wash, but by happy chance, the capital ships passed safely.

It was now, at 1940 hrs, that the signal from *K-22* was decoded in *Ithuriel*, and Cdr Leir was faced with the need to make a crucial decision. He did not know it at the time but this was a career-defining moment. He considered his options: there were three.

The first was to continue on course to the RV in the North Sea, leaving his two subordinate submarines to be cared for by ships further back in the force; although which ships they would be and on whose command they would act was an unknown. If he was to go on, then Adm Beatty's fleet would only be deficient by two submarines.

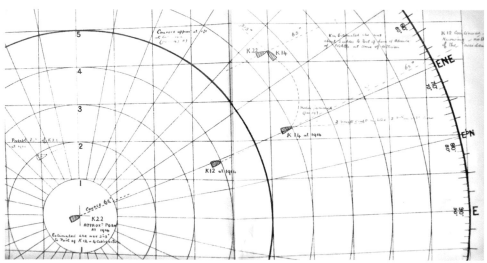

This illustrative chart was produced in evidence at the Court of Inquiry. It shows the sequence of the first collision between *K-22* and *K-14*. *K-14* altered course at 1914 hrs and was 'Not under command' for about six minutes. In that time her Captain estimated that she had moved about two cables to port of her intended course. This put her in line with *K-22* (de Burgh), which, although correctly steering 65°, was to port of *K-14*'s (Harbottle) original track (see middle left of the chart). The precise time of the collision is unclear, but it was between 1917 and 1920 hrs. *(National Archives)*

His second option was to pass command to the senior of his remaining captains and return to the collision with *Ithuriel* alone.

His third option was to turn the 13th SF around and return, as a formation, to the site of the collision. *K-14* and *K-22* were, indisputably, under his command and his responsibility. If Leir turned back, the entire flotilla would be removed from the exercise, but then it was *only* an exercise.

It is appropriate at this point to consider, briefly, what manner of man Ernest William Leir was. He was born in 1883 and was approaching his 35th birthday. He was the son of a clergyman, the Rector of Ditcheat in Somerset, near Bath. He came from a line of clergymen, and several of his ancestors had previously had the living of Ditcheat. As a consequence the Leir family was well established and well known in the West Country. Ernest had married his wife Muriel at the young age of 22. Without doubt he was one of the stars of the submarine service and to date had had a 'good war'. He had previously commanded the submarine *E-4* with great dash.

A report on him said,

Has been the senior submarine commander of 8th Flotilla since the outbreak of war and has been continuously employed in operations on the enemy's coast. All his work has been most ably carried out and his resourcefulness, coolness and keenness have been a splendid example to all in the flotilla: he

K-22 originally launched as *K-13*. She had foundered, in Jan 1917, was raised and renamed *K-22*.

rescued *Defender*'s whole crew[5] off Heligoland Bight on 28 August 1914; sank an armed trawler 22 July 1915; captured a further trawler in September 1915.

Rear Adm A.H. Christian, the same officer who had lost his three cruisers to Weddigen on 22 September, was in command of elements of the British fleet at the battle of Heligoland Bight just six days later. It was he who, formally, 'Mentioned in Dispatches' Lt Cdr Ernest Leir.

Leir was awarded the Distinguished Service Order (DSO) in 1916 and was invested by the King in June 1917. His citation reads in part, 'In recognition of services in enemy waters. He has made 17 cruises in enemy waters during which he has repeatedly been in action with Zeppelins, seaplanes and submarines. One of the latter he sank.'

His reporting officers had all commented in similar terms, describing him in his service record as 'a splendid s/m commander', 'plenty of dash', 'exceedingly reliable and resourceful', 'zealous, reliable and very capable', 'particularly good under adverse circumstances', 'a good seaman…possesses tact and good judgment…sound administrative ability'. This is the profile of a well-above-average officer.

His family genealogical website adds that 'He was a bit of a rogue.' On what basis the family would say this is not known. It may be that a kinder interpretation would be that he was a strong personality and something of a character. It appears that his idea of fun was always to carry just one cigarette in his packet. He may have thought this was fun, but his nicotine-addicted friends were less likely to be charmed. In their book *HM Submarines in Camera*, J.J. Tall and Paul Kemp commented upon Leir, saying, '*E-4* was commanded by one of the great characters of the submarine service. Lieutenant E.W. Leir, known as the "Arch thief" who plundered His Majesty's Navy of anything portable and of whom it was said that only his DSC [*sic*] was earned honestly!'

His turnout was a subject of some mirth in the submarine service, and an in-house broadsheet first warned fellow submariners of Leir's single cigarette ploy, and then commented,

We extend our sincere sympathy to Commander Leir over his recent promotion. He will now, we fear, have to buy a new cap and monkey jacket, unless – happy thought – Goldman has some of these articles still in stock. Messrs Gieves are believed to have replied to his enquiry as to 'Whether it would be possible to adapt existing uniforms' to his new rank, by saying, 'That if any part of the same (uniform) were to be pierced by a needle the whole must inevitably fall into bits.'

Despite his apparent idiosyncrasies, Ernest Leir was an effective commander and a capable seaman. His ability and personal skills are not in doubt, and his decision was entirely predictable.

The reference on the photograph to '15 patrols' is inaccurate. His MID mentions '17'.

To Leir his moral responsibility was clear, and having considered all of the factors he signalled his attendant submarines *K-11*, *K-17* and *K-12* to turn about in succession. Although the decision was taken quickly, the executive command was not given until 2010 hrs, by which time *Ithuriel* and her three subordinate submarines were about twenty nautical miles to the east. It would take about an hour to return to the point of the collision.

The second collision, 1943 hrs

Further to the west at 1941 hrs the weather had closed in and the appearance of lights had caused the OOW to call the Captain of *Inflexible* to the bridge.

The ship was close to the Isle of May, and the Captain, Navigating Officer and the OOW in *Inflexible* now saw a bright white light emerging from the mist. They concluded, incorrectly as it happened, that this was a stern light[6] of *Indomitable*, having, until then, lost touch with the ship directly ahead. Almost immediately they saw a green light indicating the starboard side of a ship.

It was dangerously close.

Inflexible put her helm hard-a-port; the ship started to answer to the helm and heeled, and the engines were put full astern. In the wardroom, cutlery laid for dinner cascaded onto the deck. Loose gear elsewhere in the ship – there is always some – rolled away. The avoiding action was too late, and *Inflexible* (Hawksley) struck *K-22*, (de Burgh), a participant in the initial collision, a 'glancing blow' at

Lieutenant Ernest Leir in working dress, about 1910. He was notoriously 'scruffy', and as this photograph shows, the reputation was well earned. *(Leir family website)*

an angle of 30°. Further severe damage was wreaked on the unfortunate *K-22*, and thirty feet of her bows were peeled back, causing them to protrude at 90°. Nevertheless, the gods smiled on the boat that night, because had a ship the size and weight of *Inflexible* hit the submarine square on then she would have ridden over the top of the smaller vessel, crushed her and sent her straight to the bottom, with massive loss of life.

K-22 scraped down the side of *Inflexible,* now even more badly wounded, but still afloat. Capt Hawksley of *Inflexible* did not linger. Although he had been involved in a collision with a small, vulnerable and friendly ship he merely called for a damage report. Finding that his ship was unscathed and content that any rescue work could be left to others, he was soon back up at full power at 21½ knots in hot pursuit of *Indomitable* – which by now had disappeared into the mist to the north-east. This was at 1943 hrs, just after Cdr Leir was made aware of the accident between *K-22* and *K-14*, while he and the remainder of his flotilla continued to steam broadly east.

The Captain of *K-22* had immediate problems. The first of these was to restore buoyancy to his boat, and to this end he dumped 150 tons of fuel and water. This measure helped to keep his boat afloat. She was not seaworthy but so far had survived. Her crew must have wondered what was coming next. They knew that, having seen the 2nd BCS disappear into the mist to the east, the arrival of *Fearless* and the 12th SF was imminent. Behind that flotilla the three battleships of the 5th BS were also approaching at high speed, through the mist, and on about the same heading.

It was a bleak prospect.

By 2010 hrs Cdr Leir, leading the remnants of his flotilla, had turned 16 points[7] and was now heading south-west up the Firth of Forth on a track that would eventually cause him to cross the track of HMS *Fearless* and the 12th SF, which was leading the remainder of the Rosyth force.

The scene was being set for further disaster.

At 2017 hrs *Ithuriel* spotted the navigation lights of *Australia*, *New Zealand* and *Indomitable*. He passed close by at three cables' distance on their starboard side, but very narrowly escaped collision with their attendant destroyers. This was another catastrophe in the making, but by chance it was avoided. There was a discernible pause and then Cdr Leir signalled the flag officer in *Australia* at 2040 hrs,

Submarines *K-12*[8] and *K-22* have been in collision and are holed forward. I am proceeding to their assistance with 13th Submarine Flotilla. Position 18 miles east magnetic from May Island.

The technology of the day was rudimentary, and this message was not received until 2120 hrs, by which time it had long been overtaken by events. *Ithuriel*, unaware that her message had not been received, altered course a little south

HMS *Inflexible*, an Invincible-class battlecruiser, 17,250 tons, launched in 1908. *(City of Glasgow Archive)*

of west to south 65° west. *K-11* was followed by *K 17* about half a mile further astern. *K-12* followed faithfully after *K-17*.

After a few minutes on this new track, an officer in *Ithuriel* and a lookout in *K-11* spotted a white light and a red port light ahead. Although they did not know it at the time, these were the lights of HMS *Fearless* (Little).

The third collision, 2032 hrs

Meanwhile, in *Fearless* they had no knowledge that the 13th SF had reversed its course, nor, initially, did they know that *Ithuriel* and her submarines were intent on crossing ahead of her. On seeing the steaming lights and green lights of three vessels fine on her port bow, *Fearless* acted in accordance with the normal 'Rule of the Road': she held to her course, and the first two ships (*Ithuriel* and *K-11*) duly crossed the bow of *Fearless* and her flotilla, in relative safety.

This had been an important decision point for Leir. On sighting *Fearless* he should have realized that what was safe for *Ithuriel* was likely to be hazardous for the submarines bringing up the rear of his flotilla.

All attention was now focused on the third unidentified ship. This was *K-17* (Hearn), and behind her was *K-12*, commanded by Bower.

Capt Charles Little had every reason to suppose that this unknown submarine would also seek to follow its flotilla leader and cross his bows, but only if it was safe to do so. As *Fearless* closed on the third vessel (*K-17*, Hearn) it became apparent that the two ships were converging dangerously, and it was the clear responsibility of the submarine to alter course in order to pass the larger ship port to port. However, as the submarine held its track, it became clear that she would not have time to cross the bows of *Fearless* and that a collision was inevitable. Capt Little ordered, 'Hard-a-port and full astern.' At the same time he made a signal by his siren that he was undertaking this emergency procedure.

It was too late.

Fearless, all 17,250 tons of her, and still with considerable headway, struck *K-17* on her starboard side at the foremost bulkhead of the wardroom. The impact wreaked serious structural damage to both vessels. It was 2032 hrs. *K-12* was following in the track of *K-17.*

The impact had been massive. In *K-17* the pressure hull was holed, and Lt Jackson, the First Lieutenant, who had been at his ease in the wardroom, heard the order, 'Close all watertight doors.' Jackson ran to the control room and, with Leading Seaman Westbrook, attempted to close one of the doors. Very soon after that came the order to abandon ship. Most of the crew scrambled out of the submarine and onto the casing. *K-17* was now down by the head and sinking lower all the time. There was no doubt that the boat was lost. The crew moved anxiously nearer to the stern, and then many jumped into the water. *Fearless* herself, very badly damaged and down by the bows, had suffered no fatal casualties but lowered her boats, and in the illumination of a searchlight the search for survivors started.

Kimbell, the bronchial signalman, had been on his way back to his bunk from the heads when *Fearless* struck. An immediate consequence was that the lights all went out, and in that Stygian setting Kimbell heard the order, 'Close watertight doors.' He then heard the bone-chilling sound of clips being put over doors at either end of the passage in which he was standing.

He was a dead man.

He had the coolness of mind to realize that, fitted to a bulkhead in that passage, was a large spanner. He felt his way through the darkness and by happy chance got his hands on the spanner. He moved aft, now a significantly 'uphill' journey, and beat on the firmly closed, watertight door. A voice from the other side enquired, 'Who's there?' One wonders why it should have mattered 'who'.

Counter to all safety regulations, the watertight door was opened and Kimbell squeezed through into the next compartment. Among the men there was the engineer officer, possibly Lt Cecil Warde. The officer was a resourceful man and he decided that he would utilize the high-pressure air cylinders fitted in the immediate vicinity. He explained quietly to the others that what he intended to do was to release the high-pressure air and, by so doing, apply pressure to the hatch above. He instructed one man to mount the ladder into the hatch space and, when the order came, to release the clips holding the hatch closed and watertight. The air was released and the pressure built up. Judging the time to be right, he gave the order and the clips were released. The hatch flew open and the men inside made their way to the surface. This should have been the happy ending.

But it was not to be.

The fourth collision, approximately 2036 hrs

Two cables[9] astern of *Fearless*, the captain of *K-4*, Cdr David Stocks, responded to the urgent 'D's coming from the siren of *Fearless* and meaning 'My engines are going astern'.[10] Stocks too put his engines astern and brought his boat to a stop, but *K-3*, under the command of Lt Cdr Herbert Shove, and the next in line, drove on and only narrowly missed the stationary *K-4* on her port side. *K-3* stopped about three cables further east.

The OOW in *K-6* (Layton) was Lt Sandford, and he altered course slightly to starboard to clear *K-12*, the last in line of the 13th Flotilla, which had been on a course to cross his bows but had now prudently altered to pass the 12th SF port to port. Sandford had been assiduously following the stern light of *K-3*, but now, momentarily, he lost it. Then a light appeared directly ahead of *K-6*, and assuming that the light was *K-3*, he took station on it. It was with quickly mounting horror that he realized that the light was not a ship or boat under way.

It was a stationary vessel lying broadside on. It was *K-4*.

Cdr Layton immediately took control from Sandford, but it was too late – far too late – and, despite *K-6* going full astern, she still had sufficient way on to be absolutely lethal. At 2036 hrs the 1,800 tons of *K-6* struck *K-4* by the after superstructure. It was as a knife plunging into the side of a long French loaf. The entire bulk and steam-driven energy of *K-6* was focused on her sharp prow, and

The damaged bow of HMS *Fearless* after its collision with *K-17*.

this sliced, cruelly, into *K-4*, severing her into two pieces. The two parts of *K-4* started to separate, and there was no sign of any of her crew.

K-6 went astern and detached herself from her mortally wounded sister ship. The withdrawal of *K-6* removed any support to the stricken submarine and served only to hasten the demise of *K-4*, which then sank almost immediately. Layton and Stocks were direct contemporaries and they had joined *Britannia* together in 1899. They knew each other very well indeed, and as is the nature of the armed forces, they competed professionally and cheerfully with each other. Nevertheless they had a personal relationship, and this added a degree of poignancy to the situation.

Lt Cdr Athelston Fenner would have been in *K-6* had chance not reappointed him, all so recently, to *K-4*. Now he died alongside his new shipmates, the names of many he still did not know, struck down by his former ship: such is the cruel hand of Fate.

The fifth collision, approximately 2038 hrs

Matters did not end with the terminal damage to *K-4*, because *K-7*, the last in line of the 12th SF, having taken no avoiding action, then passed over the sinking *K-4*,

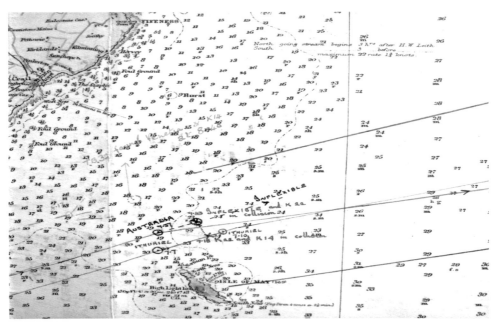

This original chart was also produced for the Court of Inquiry. It shows the juxtaposition of the Isle of May, the sites of the first two collisions and the Fife coast. It also illustrates the course alteration of the 2nd BCS ordered by the Flag in *Australia* at 1937 hrs but not followed by *Inflexible*. *Venetia* stood by *K-14*, and it can be seen that by 2048 hrs both vessels had moved some way north, away from the position of the original collision, to a position of relative safety. *MTB 32* arrived on the scene at the same time. (*National Archives*)

touching the doomed boat on the way. This would have been the *coup de grâce*, but *K-4* was already done for, and the collision did not materially alter the course of events other than to throw the judgement of the Captain of *K-7* into question. This was Lt Cdr S.M.G. Gravener. Gravener hove to, and Capt Little in *Fearless* remarked later that, 'Gravener handled *K-7* excellently in the search for survivors.'

In the meantime the survivors of *K-17*, George Kimbell among them, had been in the water for about fifteen minutes and their rescue was imminent when there arrived on the scene the three vast ships of the 5th BS and their screen of destroyers. By now *K-7* was assisting in the rescue of the crew of *K-17*, and a number of the crew were huddled on the upper deck, while the remainder were still in the icy water.

There is an ample amount of sea room north and east of the Isle of May. The island is about five miles away from Anstruther on the Fife coast, and once past the island a ship is into the enormous tract of the North Sea.

The three great battleships of the 5th BS, holding to their ordered course, now bore down on the confusion at high speed. These ships, among the mightiest in the world, were highly likely to add to the night's butcher's bill, and any vessel stationary in their path was at extreme risk. By happy and incredible chance they thundered by, missing all of the smaller craft by a minimal distance, but creating a massive wash, which served to throw the remainder of the crew of *K-17* off the casing and into the sea to join their shipmates. The 5th BS sailed on, oblivious of the carnage it had just passed, and merely bemused by the proliferation of lights it left behind. It followed *Courageous, Australia, New Zealand, Indomitable* and *Inflexible* to the rendezvous with Admiral Beatty in the North Sea.

Kimbell, of *K-17*, spoke about it in 1986, when he was interviewed by A.S. Evans at the age of 90:[11]

> Cries from the others had ceased and I seemed to be on my own now. I saw a small white light. I did not know how far away it was nor what it was. I set out floating and swimming towards it as well as my strength and confidence would permit. Then I saw the heavy white bow waves of the battleships with their escorting destroyers. Being a signalman of some experience I knew the distance between the big ships and their escorts and the distance between the ships in line ahead. Putting all my remaining strength and willpower to the test, I succeeded in getting between the ships. I stayed in that area until they had passed me safely.

At first this account by Kimbell's sounds authentic enough, but the reality of a man swimming in a cold sea and being able to dodge between two lines of fast-moving ships does not bear close examination. Kimbell talked a good game, but he was, probably, just very lucky.

The remainder of the crew of *K-17* were not so fortunate, and they were directly in the track of the Battle Squadron's escorting destroyer screen, which drove over them, either mangling their limbs in their racing screws, crushing them with their sharp bows or sucking the unfortunate men under the water in the turbulence of their wake. Almost the entire crew of *K-17* was lost in moments.

This night was already a disaster but it had now become a catastrophe.

Cdr Stocks's boat *K-4* had sunk, in two pieces, to the ocean floor. Fifty-five officers and men went down with her – the entire ship's company. No fewer than thirteen of this boat's company were holders of the Distinguished Service Medal (DSM), a remarkably high proportion.[12] The Spice boys would not be going back to leafy Wimbledon Common, and they joined Electrical Artificer Ralph Hill in death, along with William Dangerfield and Thomas Young. At No. 1 Prison Quarters, a bleak place at the best of times, the news would have devastated Young's parents.

The boats of *K-7* searched diligently, but between them could only find an officer and eight men from *K-17*. It was a poor harvest, as many more had been thrown violently into the sea by the wash of the 5th BS. These unfortunates were never seen again. George Kimbell, one of the survivors, described his rescue as follows:

> Unfortunately, during my time [in the water], I had to stay in thick fuel oil for so long that, being in my birthday suit I was black all over and I had swallowed so much oil that I was full up to my throat in it. But I was concerned with the white light. It was still there and seemed much nearer. I was doing my best to swim and float on my back and was in that position when a light was shone on my face and I heard someone cry, 'There's another one.' A rope was thrown to me. I grasped it but hadn't the strength to hold it for more than a second or two. Another rope was thrown. This time it fell across my chest. As I held it something came into my mind that I had learned in my training: pass the rope round your body and under the arms and twist it around its own part. This I did and in this way I was hauled aboard *K-7*.

One officer and nine men was a meagre harvest from the sea that night, and sadly, one of the men died soon after his thirty-minute immersion in the water. *Fearless* also launched her boats in the search for survivors, but they found none – only flotsam. The first lieutenant, Lt Cdr Maltby, aided by the carpenter, Mr C.A. Pike, did sterling work to ensure the safety of the ship, which was briefly in doubt, as *Fearless*, despite her bulk, was badly disabled. About 30 ft of her bow was a crumpled mass, and she could not steam ahead for fear of breaching further watertight compartments and sinking.

At 2115 hrs the ships that had played a part in the events of the night were lying stationary, with lights burning, in a position where they no longer had the protection of the Firth of Forth. They were on the fringe of the dangerous North Sea. This was not a place to loiter, and the captains of all the ships and boats

The Isle of May as seen from Pittenweem on a lovely Fife evening. The site of the battle was approximately above the television aerials in the middle of the picture *(Ian Mills)*

realized that they were very exposed to attack by any submarine, perhaps the one spotted some eight hours earlier by the sea plane.

Capt Charles Little in *Fearless* recognized the vulnerability of his flotilla. He ordered *K-6* and *K-7* to return to Rosyth, and reported that his ship was flooded forward. Given the severe damage to the bows of *Fearless*, her Captain attempted to return to harbour stern first, but this proved to be impractable, and so very slowly, at barely 3½ knots, *Fearless* set off on an ignominious return to harbour.

Elsewhere, in the now congested waters north-east of the Isle of May, HMS *Venetia*, one of the destroyer screen, had taken the damaged *K-14* in tow. Lt Cdr Arthur Wright, her Captain, was a skilled ship handler, and his talents were sorely needed that night. His successful recovery of *K-14* drew plaudits from the Naval establishment when the story of the night's events was finally pieced together.

The public record makes no mention of the many destroyers that escorted the Rosyth force. There were at least twenty of them, and they added to the confusion without actually participating in the events of the evening. Only HMS *Venetia* was an active player on this maritime stage.

The battleships having passed by, *K-22* had sea room, and although able to manoeuvre, she could make barely 3 knots. This speed was dependent upon the strength of her forward watertight doors, her bow having been lost. Escorted by an armed trawler which stood by her, she too made her way painfully back to Rosyth and the inevitable post mortem.

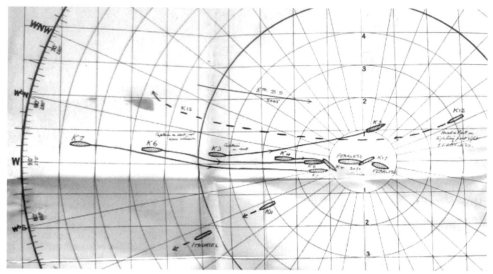

This chart is another of the originals that were produced at the direction of the Court of Inquiry, and it shows the sequence of the third, fourth and fifth collisions. It illustrates the courses and juxtaposition of all of the ships at about 2045 hrs. It is clear that the 5th BCS could, so very easily, have been deeply involved and made the situation even worse. As it was, its destroyer screen passed over and killed many of the initial survivors of *K-17*. The course steered by *K-12* was prudent, and, quite correctly, she passed *Fearless* and the 12th SF port to port. However, in doing so her track and that of *K-3* crossed. This was yet another potential collision, though fortunately avoided. *(National Archives)*

Meanwhile Vice Adm Evan-Thomas, his force severely depleted by at least twelve ships, continued north-east to rendezvous with Adm Beatty. Desirable as fleet submarines were thought to be, there would now be none on this exercise. Signal traffic was intense, but it served only to confuse the recipient, as each sender had a different view of the situation. The exercise EC1 went ahead in an abbreviated and anticlimactic form, but predictably it found no Germans to fight.

Notes

1. Today, the distance between formations is measured from the leading ship of one squadron to the leading ship of the squadron astern – thus the clear water between two formations a nominal five nautical miles apart is, perhaps, as little as four nautical miles. The likelihood is that this was also the case in 1918.
2. In 1918 helm orders were different, and the supposition was that the rudder was activated by a tiller. Therefore to move to port (left in layman's terms) the tiller would be pushed to starboard (right). Hard-a-starboard would therefore move the ship's head to port. This is all rather confusing. The convention changed in the 1920s. Now 'hard-a-starboard' means just that!

3. It was reasonable for *K-22* to suppose that *K-12* was the other vessel because that was the boat directly in line ahead of *K-22*.
4. The evidence given at the court of inquiry said 'west'. This makes no sense, and the text has been amended to read 'east'.
5. This is inaccurate. HMS *Defender*, a destroyer, had launched her boats to rescue survivors from the German torpedo-boat *V-187* when the enemy cruiser *Stettin* appeared and brought her under effective fire. *Defender* had to withdraw from the scene and was obliged to abandon her boats. Leir in *E-4*, who had observed the action, surfaced and took aboard three wounded German sailors and the crews of the two boats.
6. Stern lights were blue.
7. There are 32 points of the compass, each of 11.25°. Thus 16 points is 180°, and Leir had reversed his course back into the teeth of the remainder of the force.
8. Based on the best information available at the time.
9. A cable is one-tenth of a nautical mile. A nautical mile is 6,080 feet, and therefore a cable is about 200 yards.
10. A ship sounding one long blast and two short blasts on its siren is indicating that its engines are going astern, but it does not follow that the ship has sternway.
11. This account is taken from *Above us the waves*, by A.S. Evans.
12. In contrast, *K-17* numbered only one DSM among its ranks.

CHAPTER FOUR

Court of Inquiry

The situation at 2120 hrs was that two submarines, *K-4* and *K-17*, had sunk with only eight survivors. HM Submarines *K-6*, *K-14*, *K-22* and the light cruiser HMS *Fearless* were all damaged. HMS *Inflexible* had suffered minor damage. There had not been a single German in sight throughout this mayhem. This was not the Royal Navy's finest hour, and everyone knew it.

Everyone also knew there would have to be a reckoning, but from this moment on the events of 31 January 1918 were to be hidden from public gaze under the blanket of 'Secret' for seventy-six years and until all the participants were dead.

The Royal Navy moved swiftly to establish who had done what to whom, and when and why. The period since the 'battle'[1] had seen considerable signal traffic, and urgent telegrams had been exchanged between all of the principal naval commands concerned. There were questions to be asked and explanations given.

In barely four days a Court of Inquiry was ordered to convene aboard the battleship HMS *Orion* under the presidency of Rear Adm W.E. Goodenough CB MVO,[2] the flag officer of the 2nd BCS, who flew his flag in that ship. William Goodenough was a high-profile officer, and his selection to head the Court of Inquiry was as sound as it was predictable. The navigator of *Orion*, Cdr (N)[3] O.H. Dawson, Capt W.M. Ellerton CB, the Captain of the battleship HMS *Erin* and his navigator, Lt Cdr (N) W.C.T. Tancred, were the others appointed to conduct the investigation.

It was quite clear that this enquiry was going to focus its attention on navigational matters; nevertheless, the two navigating officers were not formally members of the Court. They were termed 'Associate Members', and they did not sign the proceedings, so the responsibility for the attribution of blame – if there was to be any – rested on Goodenough and Ellerton.

Statements in writing had been called for immediately after the event from all the participants, and this written evidence was to hand when the Court assembled. Witnesses were summoned and any number of officers searched their consciences.

The Court of Inquiry opened at 0945 hrs on Tuesday 5 February 1918, and it sat for five days. There had been five separate collisions involving a total of eight ships to be considered. These collisions were between:

K-22 and *K-14*
HMS *Inflexible* and *K-22*
HMS *Fearless* and *K-17*
K-6 and *K-4*
K-7 and *K-4*

There was a formidable list of witnesses to examine. The captains, navigators, OOWs and, in some cases, the helmsmen of many of the ships in the Rosyth force were to be called and in the process help the Court to piece together a coherent narrative and time frame. The two navigating officers on the Court were instructed to produce a comprehensive chart showing the movement of all the ships.[4] For this they had to assemble their logs and analyse the helm orders given at any time. This could be termed 'forensic navigation'. It is these charts, prepared by Cdr Dawson and Lt Cdr Tancred, that appear in this book. The examination of the witnesses was left to the two senior officers.

Rear Adm Goodenough determined the sequence in which witnesses would be heard, and he made a start with:

Cdr (N) W.E. Cornabe RN, HMAS *Australia*
Lt Cdr (N) B.K. Boase RN, HMS *Inflexible*
Lt (N) G.J.A. Miles RN, HMS *Fearless*
Lt D.A. Casey DSC RNR, HMS *Ithuriel*

These officers were all called and formally cautioned. The cautioning process, although no more than part of a well-tried routine for such enquiries, would nevertheless have concentrated their minds wonderfully, and they were instructed to assist the two 'Associate Members' of the Court in the production of their master chart.

The first witness to give direct evidence was, predictably, Cdr Ernest William Leir. He had been in command of 13th SF, and one of his boats (*K-17*) had sunk and two (*K-14*, *K-22*) had been badly damaged. There were questions for him to answer, but as is the custom in these matters, the whole affair was conducted in a non-confrontational, almost conversational manner.

Leir started by telling the Court that his flotilla was anchored in Burntisland[5] Roads waiting to take his place astern of HMS *Courageous*. He then led those present though the events as he saw them:

At about 1845 hrs I lost sight of *Courageous* stern light and increased speed to 17 knots and again to 19 knots at 1854. At 1907 hrs May Island light was S

20° W. At 1910 hrs I altered course to N 89° E. At about 1945 hrs I received a wireless message from *K-22* to the effect that she had been in collision with *K-12*. The first part of the signal started with NOVA SCOTIA,[6] a wrong group having apparently been used, and my first impression was that a steamer called *Nova Scotia* had been in collision with *K-12*.

One does have sympathy for Leir, as the first information he received was clearly corrupted and the foundations for confusion were firmly laid. Leir went on to say that at 2000 hrs, while heading N 89° E, he made a signal to his subordinates, ordering them to turn in succession 16 points to starboard. He gave the executive order at 2010 hrs, and commented that his three submarines changed course in good order. He switched on navigation lights to full brilliancy. *Ithuriel* and the 13th SF were now closing on the eastward-bound force at a combined speed of about 36 knots, and in only eight minutes, at 2018 hrs, *Ithuriel* passed *Australia*, about three cables distant on the starboard beam.

Leir then got to the meat of his direct involvement by saying that, having by now passed the 2nd BCS,

> I started to haul out to the southward. Before swinging more than a few degrees I sighted the navigation lights of a destroyer right ahead. I ported my helm [to turn to starboard and pass the other ship port to port as the 'rule of the road' requires] and swung to starboard not more than a point [11¼°].

He returned to his original course, but then saw the lights of a second destroyer, so he steered under her stern and altered course to S 65° W. A further alteration at 2045 hrs to N 88° W followed. It was 2100 hrs before *Ithuriel* sighted the lighthouse on May Island bearing N 75° W, and it was only at 2115 hrs that Leir was able to close on *K-14*. This was just over an hour since the accident, and during this period the remainder of the 13th Flotilla had steamed about 21 nautical miles. Leir said, 'I ascertained that *Venetia* had successfully taken *K-14* in tow and that *K-22* had proceeded to harbour. I stood by her [*K-14*]. She was floating with very small buoyancy and had a large number of her crew on board.

It must be presumed that, if *Ithuriel* was standing by *K-14*, his other three submarines were close by and stationary. Cdr Leir was questioned by Rear Adm Goodenough, who, somewhat tersely, wanted to know what Ernest Leir had done to warn the remainder of the force that he was turning round. Leir produced the wireless log and said that his signal had been sent to the Vice-Admiral, Commanding Light Cruiser Force [Evan-Thomas], 'in cypher'.

William Goodenough then asked,

> When you altered course 16 points to go to the assistance of your damaged submarines what appreciation did you form of the rapidity with which the

following group or groups would come up on top of you, knowing the high speeds that obtain in modern warfare?

Leir knew that he would be asked this question or something similar. He was suitably prepared and gave a prompt reply,

I knew I was at least five miles ahead of the leading battlecruiser and I considered that it would be better for me to alter course 16 points than to break away from the line in either direction on a less alteration than this, as I considered that meeting a ship end on is the best way to avoid her.

The matter of illumination was bound to be raised, and Cdr Leir was questioned closely about the use of lights. He stated firmly that, had he used a searchlight, it would have made his navigation lights ineffective and caused confusion. It was a fact that navigation lights would have been indecipherable against searchlights, and the Court, practical seamen, did not pursue the matter.

The Court now went to the chronological order of events, and called and cautioned Cdr T.B. Harbottle, Captain of *K-14*, and Lt Cdr C. de Burgh DSO, Captain of *K-22*. It had been their original altercation that had been the overture to the greater drama that was to follow.

Harbottle gave crucial evidence – evidence of the sequence that set the train of events in motion. He advised the Court that he was proceeding at 19 knots and exactly in the wake of *K-17* when that boat slowed down and moved slightly to port. Harbottle slowed his boat and,

Suddenly, two small craft in single line ahead exhibited navigation lights, the port light being toward me two points on my starboard bow, and they were palpably moving ahead. I decided to avoid them by altering course to port and picking up my position astern of the leading boat. I ordered 'starboard 15' and immediately afterwards 'hard-a-starboard', switched on navigation lights and having swung through 3 points ordered 'amidships'. The helmsman reported the helm jammed.

This jammed helm was the key to the original collision, and predictably it was to be the subject of a very detailed examination by engineers in the naval dockyard a few days later.

Rear Adm Arthur Leveson CB, the commander of the 2nd BCS, was not able to offer much other than to reveal that he did not know how many destroyers were escorting his squadron and under his command! His evidence was delivered in the manner of a man somewhat elevated above such mundane matters as those under current review. He said that he had had a signal from *Inflexible* that reported the collision with *K-22*, in which Capt Hawksley said that 'there were plenty of vessels around to assist in the collision area and so he came on'. The Admiral said that he had detached HMS *Venetia* to assist with rescue work and he closed by making some professionally damaging, irrelevant and gratuitous remarks about the Captain of HMS *Verulam*, one of his escorts, that had no bearing on the enquiry.

Leveson may have resented Goodenough, who, although of the same rank, was considerably his junior. The transcript, when read ninety years later, does present Leveson in an unattractive light, and he comes across as a pompous ass.

The flag lieutenant-commander to the Rear Admiral of the 2nd BCS, and serving in that capacity in HMAS *Australia*, was one Lt Cdr P.A. Warre. When called he said that the first *Australia* knew of any accident was at 1939 hrs, when an Aldis lamp made the signal, 'Stand by we have been in collision.' Warre estimated the ship making the signal to be, 'Half a mile ahead and just off the port bow.' At 1938 hrs May Island was abeam of *Australia* to starboard. He went on to say that, at 1954 hrs, a priority signal, in code, was sent to the 5th BS, 'Vessel in distress in path of fleet due north May Island. Destroyer standing by.'

The navigator of *Australia*, Cdr W.E. Cornabe, endorsed all of the above and added that the course was altered, at 1937 hrs, to S 86° E in order to follow a line down 'the southern half of area 10 middle'.[7]

Capt J.R.P. Hawksley CB CVO, the Captain of HMS *Inflexible*, attended to deal with the matter of his ship's collision with *K-22*. His evidence was unsatisfactory, and the written record gives the impression that here was an officer so anxious not to commit himself that what he did say was sprinkled with caveats. He was not even prepared to say, specifically, which part of his ship had made contact with *K-22*. Hawksley served only to confirm that he and his officers were confused by the various lights that appeared ahead of them. He agreed that he was steaming at 16 knots, but had given orders to increase to 21 knots just before the collision. He estimated his speed at impact as 'about 18 knots', and said that, despite taking late evasive action and reversing his engines, he could not avoid *K-22*, which he struck with his port side, eventually agreeing that the point of impact was around his paravane chains.[8] The captain referred two key questions to his navigating officer, and gave the impression that he was badly briefed. He averred that at no time had he lost sight of *Indomitable*, and the court did not pursue him on this matter. The examination of Hawksley was, at best, cursory.

Hawksley's failure to stop after the collision with *K-22* to ascertain what help he could provide was not raised. Presumably his view, expressed in the signal to the 2nd BCS at the time, 'that there were sufficient ships in the collision area', was satisfactory. His conduct appears to have been acceptable – at least no criticism of him was ever voiced publicly. At this distance the impression is that Hawksley was given an easy passage. He was the Captain of a capital ship, but although *K-22* did not sink and she suffered no casualties, Hawksley was not to know that – because he did not wait to find out.

Lt Cdr (N) B.K. Boase amplified his Captain's evidence by saying that *Inflexible* was abeam May Island at 1941 hrs at a distance of 1½ miles. He saw 'a white masthead light' fine on the port bow 2½–3 cables ahead. Helm orders swung the ship 'three or four points, but the collision with *K-22* was at an angle of about 30°.' This was at 1943 hrs.

Boase made the point that the change of course ordered by Rear Admiral 2nd BCS from N 82° E to S 86° E had not been reported, and he agreed that, as a result, *Inflexible* was to port of the track desired by the admiral. If *Inflexible* was steaming at 16–18 knots just before her collision with *K-22*, as Hawksley said, then she would have been a little less than the 400 yards off track to port estimated earlier. Precisely how far to port was never clearly established, and as it was an important factor, the Court of Inquiry seemed to have missed a trick. It was probably in the range 250–350 yards, but obviously enough to put her on a collision course with *K-22*.

The President interjected to read a signal intercepted by *Inflexible*,

From: 2nd BCS
To: 5th BS
Priority. Have just passed *Ithuriel* and 3 subs inward bound time 2025

Lt The Hon John Bruce, who had been OOW in *Inflexible*, reiterated everything that the court already knew, but confirmed that he had had a signal as to speed from the Flag, but had received nothing relating to course; accordingly he had held his head at N 82° E.

Lt Laurence Dickinson, OOW in *K-22*, was called and gave evidence that at 1917 hrs his boat was steaming at 19 knots. He was accompanied on the bridge by the quartermaster, a signalman and a lookout when he saw an assortment of lights, up close and four or five points on his starboard bow. He saw a vessel crossing his bow from starboard to port. He altered course to port but the head had swung only about two points when the collision with *K-14* followed almost immediately. Dickinson said that after the collision *K-22* was stationary and was passed by a number of ships, close to and on both sides.

The flag commander to Commander-in-Chief, Coast of Scotland, was called and identified himself as Cdr W.R.W. Kettlewell. He was asked to specify the arrangements when a large force was proceeding to sea. Kettlewell replied that on receipt of the 'Gate signal' the Extended Defence Officer (EDO) Inchkeith[9] would be warned in detail of how many ships were making the passage and at what time. He would then warn all of his patrol vessels.

The court enquired how many patrol vessels there were between 1800 and 2000 hrs on 31 January. Kettlewell advised that there were three motor torpedo boats (MTB). Those vessels were Nos 25, 28 and 32, and, in addition, there were two yachts. He added that there were 'probably two trawlers reinforcing the yacht to the south of May Island'. This vague and unsatisfactory 'probably' was not challenged.

The captains of the MTBs were all called. They were:

Lt R.L. Alexander RNR	MTB *25*
Lt R. Gill RNR	MTB *28*
Lt R.T. Park RNR	MTB *32*

These young officers could add little of value other than explaining that they were sent to assist *K-12*, *K-14* and *K-22*. When asked, Park said that at 2000 hrs visibility to the west was two miles and to the east three-quarters of a mile.

The examination of Acting Engineer Lt T. Garden of *K-14* provided absolutely no information other than that the steering gear had never jammed before, was now working perfectly and no explanation could be found for the mishap. Rear Adm Goodenough was not going to settle for this trite reply, and he made a request, through Cdr Leir, that the gear be stripped from the boat, dismantled and subjected to very close examination by dockyard experts and engineering officers.

This was an interesting procedure, and one might have assumed that the President could order any sort of examination he chose on his own considerable authority without having to refer to a third person. However, *K-14* was still under the command of Ernest Leir, and so a service courtesy was observed. It was one to which Leir readily, and probably eagerly, acquiesced.

In the meantime AB Harold Curtis, the helmsman of *K-14*, repeated to the court the helm orders he had been given. He said that the helm was jammed for between five and seven minutes. After a moment's thought, he then revised his estimate to five minutes. These estimates of time are very imprecise and probably unimportant, but the time that elapsed was sufficient to place *K-14* in the path of *K-22*.

No time was lost in investigating the jammed helm. Within two days and on 7 February 1918, a panel of three officers reported on the steering gear of *K-14*. It was found to be in all respects functioning perfectly. The gear had been subjected to a wide range of tests but the panel could find no explanation for it jamming, and they had been unable to replicate the problem. No other K boat had ever experienced such a malfunction before and never would again.

The jamming of *K-14*'s steering was, in essence, the cause of the 'Battle of the Isle of May'. Had this machinery functioned correctly there would have been no collision with *K-22*, *Ithuriel* would not have reversed her course and *K-17* would not have been in the position of crossing the bows of *Fearless*. The circumstances would not have existed that caused *K-6* and *K-7* to collide with *K-4*. It was all highly unsatisfactory and somewhat mysterious.

Machines do not fail of their own volition and without some physical cause – but in this case no cause was ever found. The Court was at a complete loss and let the matter rest there. The failure to identify a cause for the jammed steering would have sapped the confidence of the captains of the remaining K boats and further damaged the reputation of the class.

Lt Cdr J.G. Bower, the Captain of *K-12*, threw some light on the two mysterious small craft. (They may of course have been two entirely different small craft from those seen by *K-14*.) He said that, when they appeared on his bow, at first he made to alter course, but then, seeing that they were very small[10] and moving slowly, he sounded his siren and obliged them to alter their course. They turned right round and headed off in a south-westerly direction about a cable apart.

Lt G.E.A. Jackson, the only officer to survive the sinking of *K-17*, was called, but his experience of the night's events was limited to the circumstances of his survival, and he could add nothing material to explain the loss of his boat. He was shocked by the collision and played no part in the command of the submarine thereafter. The surviving ratings were called to describe the events of that night. The men were:

Stoker Petty Officer James Stewart
Leading Seaman Frederick Bown
Signalman George Kimbell
Leading Seaman Anthony Westbrook
Stoker 1st Class Kenneth Vass
Stoker 1st Class Henry Fulcher
Stoker 1st Class Albert Dowding

Westbrook gave the most coherent evidence when he said,

At about 8.32 hrs there was an order to 'close watertight doors'. I repeated it to AB Drake. He went to the telephone and rang up aft and gives the people aft the tip like, Sir. He went to the beam tube head and repeated the order. In the act of closing the doors and an order came, 'Everyone on the upper deck.'

Dowding speculated that *K-17* had sunk 'within eight minutes'.

George Kimbell, who gave a colourful and detailed description of his escape from the doomed submarine when he spoke about it in 1986, aged 90, was a great deal less loquacious only days after the disaster. One might speculate whether or not the sixty-eight years since the sinking had served to sharpen his memory. But in 1918, within days of the events, he offered no information on the sinking, and only provided the routine facts that on 31 January he had been sick, had only four months' service in submarines and did not find his signalling duties difficult. His escape and the cool-headedness of the officer who manipulated the HP air containers, described so well to A.S. Evans,[11] surely bore the telling to the enquiry? To be fair, perhaps the court did not question him closely enough.

Two officers of the RNR were called from HMY *Shemara*, a boom defence vessel. Her function was to patrol the anti-submarine defences of the Firth of Forth. Lt J. McCullum, the Captain, said that an armed trawler had been detailed to reinforce *Shemara* on her patrol but *Culblean* did not turn up. However, HMAT *Strathella* did. McCullum added that, at 1900 hrs, he was patrolling two miles north of the Isle of May and between the island and Crail[12] when, at about 2010 hrs, he saw a red rocket followed by a white, and he knew that that indicated that something was wrong. He then saw a signal light sending a message, 'Want assistance…am sinking.'

He steered for the light, and when he got to the scene he found that he had been forestalled by two destroyers and a trawler (none of which were named). Lt A. Badman, the other RNR officer in *Shemara,* added that, at 1900 hrs, two trawlers were close to the southern end of the Isle of May and using hydrophones. He said he could not identify the vessels by name, was unable to say where *Strathella* was and he had no idea of the whereabouts of *Culblean*. He said that there were no MTBs in the vicinity, and his only intimation of a force leaving Rosyth was the presence 'of a large number of destroyers'.

The ignorance of Badman was worrying, and did not reflect well on McCullum, who, when he was questioned on the matter, cheerfully admitted that he had had a message to tell him that the fleet would sail at 1730 hrs. Questioned as to his response to this wireless message, he said that he 'kept south of a line that the fleet generally comes out'. It would seem that Badman, the only other officer in *Shemara,* was unaware of this important intelligence, and one wonders at the personal and professional relationship of these two officers serving in such a small ship.

It is surprising that William Goodenough did not 'grip' both of these officers. He was a robust, seasoned seaman who demanded high standards from his officers, and the inept performance of Badman and McCullum must surely have grated upon him. If it did then his displeasure was not expressed in Court. There is no official record of Lt McCullum being called to account for his cavalier attitude, but perhaps he had an 'interview without coffee' after he had given evidence.

Lt Cdr H.W. Shove DSO, the Captain of *K-3*, explained how close he had come to ramming *K-4* when he found her stopped in his path. He commented that he only missed ramming her by taking violent avoiding action. He remarked on the scene of confusion and the plethora of lights, and he saw *K-17* sink steeply by the bows with men standing on the stern, illuminated by searchlights trained on her after deck.

The Court questioned Lt L.F. Foley, AB N. Haley and Signalman J.W.F.G. Richards, all of *K-3*, as to the relative positions of *K-3*, *K-4* and *Fearless*. They all agreed that, when *K-3* stopped, *Fearless* was just abaft their starboard beam. Haley had been the helmsman and he gave an impression of the nature of the night when he said that the 5th BS had passed between *K-3* and *K-17*. The big ships were steaming at about 21 knots and must have looked a worrying sight to those able to see their approach from the conning towers of the various stationary submarines. A picture emerges of a cluster of stationary ships, all displaying lights and gathered into a relatively small space, in the middle of a main channel to the North Sea, and very vulnerable to attack.

Cdr Geoffrey Layton, the Captain of *K-6*, a boat that most emphatically did not avoid *K-4*, was called to explain himself.

Geoffrey Layton had made an impact on the Royal Navy soon after the outbreak of war when in command of HM Submarine *E-13*. He had been ordered to the Baltic to give support to the Russians, but ran his boat aground on the Danish Island of Saltholm. The situation took a turn for the worse when a German destroyer shelled *E-13*, killing fifteen of the crew. The Danes took exception to *E-13* taking up residence on their property, and having refloated the wrecked boat they interned Layton and the surviving fifteen members of his crew. Layton escaped from the internment camp, swam a canal, and rejoined the fleet. The loss of the submarine did not inhibit Layton's career, and, soon afterwards he took command of *K-6*.

Now he described arriving on the bridge just as the OOW, Lt Sandford, had given the order to alter course to starboard to follow *K-3* and to avoid a vessel showing her starboard light while apparently crossing the bows of *K-6* from port to starboard.[13] There was a flurry of activity on the bridge of *K-6*, Layton immediately took charge of the boat from Lt Sandford and realized that the lights he saw were of a stationary vessel in his path. Collision was inevitable, and despite the fact that, by now, the engines of *K-6* were going full astern, the boat still had considerable headway. Layton ordered that *K-6* sound her siren. He turned on all her navigation lights and directed her searchlight over the stern to warn *K-7*, which was following the same course. The warning had no effect; *K-7* held to her track, and just ahead of her *K-6* rammed *K-4* with devastating results.

Layton stated that after the impact *K-4* started to sink immediately, and 'to carry us down with her'. His engines gained sternway, and as the two boats separated *K-4* sank.

Lt Sandford had been OOW and therefore in charge of *K-6* until only a few moments before she collided with *K-4*, and he came in for some stern questioning. He was asked,

'Could you see the stern light of *K-3*?'

'Yes.'

'What appreciation did you make of the situation when you heard Ds sounding?'

'The Ds appeared to be given about four points on the starboard bow, and I took them to be a vessel towing; the weather at the time was misty.'

'Did you take any action?'

'No direct action.'

'What do you understand the significance of Ds to be?'

'I assume them to mean a vessel towing, but it did not occur to me at the time.'

'What is the significance of the signal D?'

'It may be sounded by a vessel out of control.'

Later, Sandford might regret not only his relative inaction on the night but his answers to the court in the clear light of day. The helmsman of *K-6*, Leading Seaman William Poustie, was called, and he said that despite the misty conditions and spray coming over the boat's bows, he had maintained station on *K-3* and *Fearless* without undue difficulty.

As *K-4* dipped below the surface in two pieces, *K-7*, captained by Lt Cdr S.M.G. Gravener, continued to steam in from the west. *K-7* had not responded to the warning of *K-6*, left any avoiding action until too late and drove over *K-4* between the bow and the conning tower. In the process *K-7* lightly brushed *K-4*. Technically this was a collision, but *K-7* had had no material effect on the loss of *K-4* and had not damaged herself. The court, however, did not view the matter lightly, and regarded the brush as 'a collision'.

Capt J.R.P. Hawksley of HMS *Inflexible* was recalled and stoutly averred that his ship, 'was dead astern of *Indomitable*' – this despite his having missed the order to alter course earlier.[14] Erring on the side of generosity, one could surmise that, having made the belated correction to his course, he was dead astern but with a greater gap than was desirable. Rather more realistically, the veracity of Capt Hawksley on this matter is open to question. Hawksley's assertion that he was dead astern of *Indomitable* raises the question, 'Why then did *Indomitable* not collide with *K-22*?'

Capt A.W. Craig CB, in command of HMS *Barham*, commented that he had received a signal from 2nd BCS informing him of 'a vessel in distress about two miles north of May Island'. He observed a destroyer in attendance on the vessel and said that, '*Barham* passed the scene on her port side well clear and practically abeam May Island.' The Captain went on to recount his encounter with 13th SF, and said that one of the submarines was passed very close on the starboard side.

Surgeon Lt A.T. Fleming DSO, the doctor in HMS *Fearless*, described the rescue of the few survivors of *K-17* and said that three of the men needed medical attention. One of the men was in a dire state and he was 'practically dead'. The doctor took him to the wardroom of *K-7*, but there, after intense efforts to save him, he died. His name is not recorded.

The court ascertained from Warrant Officer Telegraphist E.W. Penny that the wireless traffic on the night was sufficiently heavy to make communications very difficult. Much of this traffic emanated from the Isle of May, where there was a significant RN presence. The island is certainly large enough to support a community, and it did so for a thousand years.[15]

Acting Lt R.B. Cuthbert of the HMAT *Cave* and Skipper R. McKay[16] of HMAT *Good Hope* gave evidence that they were three to seven miles south-east of the Isle of May, and they both agreed that they had no information about a large formation of ships leaving Rosyth. Temporary Lt R. Rigby of HMAT *Culblean* said that he had been six to eight miles east of the Isle of May between 1830 and 2000 hrs, and added that he had 'six or eight trawlers with me, mine sweeping'. The two vessels closest to *Culblean* were *Strathella* and *North King*.

This statement was allowed to stand unchallenged, and Cuthbert's assertion that he had no prior knowledge of the fleet's movements pointed to crass inefficiency somewhere. The 'six to eight trawlers' is such a vague statement that once more William Goodenough could have been expected to delve deeper. He did not.

The precise whereabouts of *North King* and *Strathella* was never established.

Notes

1. From this time on these events have been immortalized as 'The Battle of the Isle of May'.
2. He had held senior command appointments in all the three major actions of the First World War – Heligoland, Dogger Bank and Jutland.
3. The initial (N) after an officer's name indicated that his specialization was 'navigation'.
4. The charts on pages 58, 66 and 70 are those they produced to aid the court.
5. This is an anchorage off the Fife village of Burntisland, and near to and east of the Forth railway bridge.
6. A prearranged code to authenticate a following message.
7. The sea between the Isle of May and the coast was divided into navigation channels marked on charts which would be well known to all navigating officers.
8. Paravanes are equipment streamed from the bows of a ship to deflect and cut the cables of moored mines.
9. A small island in the Firth of Forth just to the east of Rosyth.
10. This does not sound like a 500-ton trawler.
11. *Above us the waves*, pages 108–13.
12. A fishing village in Fife.
13. See the chart on page 70.
14. His assertion was contradicted by the chart on page 70. This was produced by the navigating officers, and it showed *Inflexible* to port of her squadron's corrected course.
15. Today it is much visited by pleasure boats from Anstruther.
16. 'Skipper' was a rank in the RN Patrol Service in the Second World War, and it probably was in the RNPS's predecessor, the Trawler Section of the RNR. McKay was presumably a civilian, under contract, and held an Admiralty warrant.

CHAPTER FIVE

The Reckoning

The Court of Inquiry closed its proceedings on 9 February 1918, having heard, in detail, from fifty-one witnesses. The general outline of the events was not in any dispute, but several issues that arose and which could have had a bearing were not followed up. For example, how far off her ordered track to port was *Inflexible* when she struck *K-22*? There was conflicting evidence as to whether or not she had *Indomitable* in sight at all times. The high probability is that she did not, and the periods when the two ships were not in visual contact, no matter how short, were when *Inflexible* strayed.

How many small vessels were abroad in the vicinity of the Isle of May that night? Temporary Lt Rigby had said that, '*Culblean* had been with six or eight trawlers mine sweeping eight miles east of the Isle of May, and *Strathella* and *North King* were closest.'

What were the names of these vessels and what were their various courses? The Court did not require the log of any of the 'six or eight trawlers', nor were their captains called for. It was with scant evidence to support the finding that the Court rushed to conclude that the <u>two</u> (*sic*) small craft were 'almost certainly *Culblean*, *Strathella* and *North King*.' That is a glib, convenient and certainly an all-embracing conclusion of doubtful accuracy. However, it did tie up a loose end quite neatly. There is no evidence whatsoever to support the finding.

The Court was nothing if not consistent, because the Captains of *Strathella* and *North King* were not called to give evidence either. The Captain of *Culblean* was not questioned at any length, and when he was, he made no reference to sighting *Ithuriel* and the 13th SF.

There were ten questions that remained unanswered despite the fifty-one witnesses and five days of investigation by experienced senior officers. These were:

- Why did the organization responsible for guarding the entrance to the Firth not know of the fleet's movements?
- Why were the Captains of *Strathella* and *North King* not questioned?
- Why were their ship's logs not examined?
- Where were *Strathella* and *North King* at the time of the initial collision?

- Why was the identity of the 'two small vessels' not firmly established?
- Why did the steering jam in *K-14*?
- Why did the jam then clear itself?
- Why was *K-22* so far out of station to port?
- Why was the Captain of *Inflexible*, whose ship struck the stationary *K-22*, considered to be blameless?
- Why was Capt Hawksley's evidence, which lacked credibility, not subjected to closer scrutiny?

The Court clearly filed these matters either under 'Too difficult' or 'Don't want to know', and no official steps were taken to resolve them. Running through all the evidence there is a thread of poor accountability. The whereabouts of any number of ships on 31 January were unknown. The exercise order, EC1, voluminous though it is, does not name ships – only formations – and it is difficult at this distance to determine just how many ships were about the King's business that night. Rear Adm Leveson, for example, did not know how many destroyers he had under command, while Lt Rigby spoke of having 'six to eight trawlers with me'. On the basis of the very loose, cavalier accounting and the lack of attention to detail, it is perhaps no great surprise that the identity of the two, anonymous, small vessels that caused *K-14* to turn to port is still open to conjecture.

The performance of the steering gear in *K-14* was crucial, and identical equipment installed in all the other boats of this class never replicated the failure experienced, albeit briefly, by *K-14*. These boats suffered far more than

- 2 -

Lieutenant Commander S. M. G. Gravener, Commanding Officer of K-7, is being informed that blame rests upon him for failure to appreciate the necessity for getting clear, thereby causing K-7 to pass over K-4, touching her as she was sinking.

ADMIRAL.

In February 1918 Admiral Beatty, no less, issued the formal notice of Lieutenant-Commander Gravener's responsibility for the collision – an incident that, in reality, had no bearing on events whatsoever. This is an extract from the file. *(Jeff Birch)* their share of serious mishaps during their unhappy time on the maritime stage, but jammed steering was not one of them.

Satisfied that it had got to the root of the matter, the Court considered its findings, and on 9 February 1918,[1] it made an initial report very soon after the conclusion of its business. This was an ill-considered decision, as Rear Adm Goodenough and Capt Ellerton rushed to judgement. Their report attributed blame, not least, to Lt Cdr C. de Burgh of *K-22* for the collision with *Inflexible*. The report stated that, 'Blame is therefore attributable to him although damage to his vessel and the circumstances in which he was placed made the position one of great difficulty.'

This was an incredibly harsh judgement, as *K-22* was badly damaged and stationary at the time of the collision. Her role in the collision was, at worst, passive, while on the other hand the battlecruiser was under way and under command. For reasons never explained the actions of *Inflexible* and her Captain did not attract the attention they deserved. The conclusion that de Burgh (*K-22*) was blameworthy was obviously reconsidered, and common sense eventually prevailed. Both Goodenough and Ellerton would have lost face over the matter, and at this distance one might think, 'Serve them right'.

In the final report, with recommendations issued on 19 February, all reference to Lt Cdr de Burgh and the collision with *Inflexible* were excised, and quite correctly too; it would have been a travesty had the captain of a crippled boat, in danger of sinking, been blamed for being struck.

The report's reference to the collision between *K-22* and *K-14*, one of the major components of the night's chain of events, placed blame on Harbottle. A collision that might have been better laid at de Burgh's door, for it was his boat that struck the disabled *K-14*. The final report read as follows:

The following action is being taken as regards the several collisions.

Collision between K-14 *and* K-22
Commander T.C.B. Harbottle of *K-14* is being informed that some responsibility for this collision rests with him in that he would have been better advised to stop and sound 'D'[2] on his siren when the helm jammed.

Collision between Inflexible *and* K-22
No action.

Collision between Fearless *and* K-17
The Vice Admiral commanding Battlecruiser Force is being directed to forward an application for the trial by Court Martial of Commander E.W. Leir DSO to the Commander-in-Chief, Coast of Scotland.

Collision between K-6 *and* K-4
Lieutenant R.D. Sandford, Officer-of-the-Watch of *K-6*, is being informed that blame is attributable to him for not at once appreciating the necessity of getting clear and for not taking action to do so on hearing 'D's sounder on the siren ahead of him.

Collision between K-7 *and* K-4
Lieutenant Commander S.M.G. Gravener, Commanding Officer of *K-7*, is being informed that blame rests upon him for failure to appreciate the necessity for getting clear, thereby causing *K-7* to pass over *K-4*, touching her as she was sinking.

It is interesting to note that although potentially the collision of *Inflexible* and *K-22* was by far the most serious one to occur, no action was to be taken (other than to remove de Burgh's name from the list of those responsible), but on the other hand, the irrelevant brush that *K-7* had with the doomed *K-4* drew down opprobrium on the head of the unfortunately named Samuel Maryon Gorton Gravener.

The performance of William Goodenough and the members of his Court of Inquiry was well below that which might have been expected. Several issues were not resolved, witnesses were permitted to give loose, inconclusive answers, and the conclusions of the Court are supported neither by the facts nor by the application of common sense. Goodenough was a very experienced and capable officer. Not the least of the unknowns in this sorry matter was why he gave such an inadequate performance as the President of the Court of Inquiry.

The evidence from their service records shows that Harbottle and Sandford were not dealt with in the same way; nor that they were dealt with 'summarily'. That is to say, they were not subject to any administrative action The process in which an accused can be dealt with 'summarily' has two objects. The first of these is to hasten the judicial system and to allow a superior officer in the chain of command to judge the case while sitting alone. In this case they could have incurred a flag officer's or Their Lordships' 'Displeasure' or even 'Severe Displeasure', they could have been removed from their ships or reprimanded. In the case of Sandford and Harbottle, no one played the part of military magistrate.

It would seem that Harbottle and Sandford, having been duly blamed, got on with the war and their lives, having suffered no penalty and with no entry being made on their records. The administration of justice in this case was more than a little hit and miss, and Gravener was unfortunate. His offence was no more than a technicality.

Although a blanket of secrecy had been thrown over the affair, King George V had been fully briefed, and on 12 February he wrote a chatty letter to Beatty[3] from Buckingham Palace. In his letter the King first said that he was able to appreciate the anxiety that North Sea convoys were causing Beatty, and he endorsed the Admiral's decision to insist on only one being at sea at a time. The King commented upon the difficulty of protecting more than one convoy, and added that, 'When a disaster occurs all the press goes mad.' So it would seem that not a lot has changed there.

King George expressed his distress on hearing, too, of the 'deplorable accident which has just occurred to the K boats in which two were sunk and four others damaged beside the loss of valuable trained officers & men'. The King went on to observe that the Grand Fleet could ill afford the loss in ships and men, as both resources were scarce. His is the only expression of regret at the loss of life that is recorded.

Changing the subject, the King said that he was pleased to note that 'the United States Squadron[4] are settling down and learning your ways'. He observed that the squadron probably had a lot to learn, but expected them to become a useful element of the Grand Fleet in due course. The winter of 1917/18 had been very severe, and the King mentioned the awful weather there, which had been full of gales and blizzards. As a sailor he felt for those men at sea in small ships. He wrote,

The running on the rocks of those two destroyers[5] in a snow storm was horrible, wonderful news that there was one survivor.

I regret to say the U-boats are giving us a bad time again at the moment & they have sunk many large ships lately, especially in the Mediterranean, which we can ill afford to lose. Roger Keys has begun well at Dover and has bagged several U-boats already. Bacon did well but was too theoretical.

In a remarkably blunt passage of the letter he agreed with Beatty that 'the way Jellicoe[6] was removed from Admiralty was unfortunate. The Prime Minister has had his knife into him for some time & wished for a change.' This unguarded observation illustrates the relationship that existed between the King and his Admiral. King George went on to comment upon the ability of Adm Rosslyn Wemyss GCB CMG MVO, who had replaced Jellicoe at very short notice on Christmas Eve 1917. In the view of the King, Wemyss would do well as he was full of common sense, would not get bogged down in detail like Jellicoe and in addition had some bright young men around him. Finally, the King, taking a broader view, expressed the hope that the changes at the top of the establishment would serve to improve the relationship between the Admiralty and the Grand Fleet.

It is evident from the tone of this letter that Beatty and the King were confidants and friends. The King was himself a sailor, and he took a very close interest in naval matters. He would have been briefed about the Court of Inquiry, and probably knew, before Leir, that the application to charge him and submit him for trial by court martial had been agreed.

Unlike Harbottle and Sandford, there was to be no easy exit for Cdr Ernest William Leir – for him life was looking bleak, and he was duly charged about ten days later as,

'Being a person subject to the Naval Discipline Act did, on the thirty-first day of January 1918, negligently or by default suffer His Majesty's Submarine *K-17* to be lost.'

Beatty wrote a revealing letter to his wife on 12 February,[7] in which he said how grateful he was to hear from her the snippets of information that she was able to pass on. He observed that opinions expressed by flag officers, or at least people who were well informed, were useful to him.

He was very dismissive of 'Old Packs',[8] and he added that he 'is soft or weak or something which prevents him from making firm decisions. For instance, he wrote to me that the disaster to the Ks had had a very shaking effect on the officers and men in the other submarines, and suggested that they should be given leave!!'

Beatty was going to have none of that, and told his wife that the men needed to be hardened and not softened. He confided that he 'had sent one lot to sea', and that the remainder would follow at the first opportunity. Beatty made an interesting remark at this point: when referring to the 'Battle of the Isle of May', he judged that, 'Lack of sea experience is the cause of most of the disasters, and that I will correct.'

He informed his wife that he had sent the 2nd Battle Squadron and 1st Battlecruiser Squadron with the 4th Light Cruiser Squadron out on a special operation which was 'quite successful'.

He continued his letter by commenting on the two men who had been closest to him, professionally, for years, and in neither case was he very complimentary. 'I don't think that I ever read such childish twaddle as that let loose by Jellicoe, in which he gives himself away painfully. Why will those who can't talk always give themselves away? It would appear that he was endeavouring to curry favour with that old arch-ruffian Jackie Fisher.'[9] Finally, Beatty ended his letter by saying that he did not expect the war to be concluded by military means, and took the view that it would depend on which side could bear the attrition longest. He said that, 'There is no reason why that should not last for many weary years.'

Leir had about six weeks to wait before he faced trial. It would have been a miserable time in his life, and he would be only too aware that, although many of his peers had sympathy for him, others believed that his actions were culpable. He was in 'open arrest', and as such his life was in suspension. He was able to invite a brother officer to act as his 'Friend,' a curiosity of the service. This 'Friend', usually an officer with some expertise in legal matters, or at the very least a person in whom the accused had confidence, helped to assemble the Defence. He acted as defending counsel during the trial.

Edward Leir invited Capt Rafe Grenville Rowley-Conwy[10] CMG of HMS *Parker* to assist him, and on 22 March 1918 the Court was convened. Leir and

Rowley-Conwy faced together a Court Martial composed of the nine captains of HMS *Neptune, Superb, Furious, Bellerophon, Indomitable, Sydney, St Vincent, Dublin*, and, very curiously indeed, Capt James Hawksley CB CVO, the Captain of *Inflexible.*

Hawksley had not been involved in the sinking of *K-17*, but he had been a key player in the night's wider activities and his ship had been in collision with *K-22*. There is every indication that this officer would hardly have come to judge Leir with a totally clear and unbiased mind, but, to be positive, perhaps he did bring to the Court an intimate appreciation of the overall situation and the prevailing conditions.

The assembly of the Court on the flagship was conducted with due ceremony as each of the members was welcomed aboard to the shrill sounds of the bosun's pipe. They were each greeted by the OOW and were then escorted below for refreshment and to meet the Judge Advocate. All the participants were in 'full fig', with decorations, medals, swords and with all their bright surfaces well polished. The ship's company of HMS *Crescent* agreed that it would be only too glad when the matter was concluded because the First Lieutenant, only too anxious to present his ship in the best possible order, had issued stringent instructions that had resulted in tedious hours cleaning and polishing.

The composition of this Court calls for a passing comment, not least that nine captains is overkill, but it could have been more, as the record shows that a further three captains had been excused attendance. Usually five officers are judged to be sufficient for a court martial dealing with an officer. The fact that the president was of the same rank as the members is allowable but relatively unusual. The prosecuting officer was Capt E.V. Underhill, who commanded HMS *Temeraire* and had done so at Jutland, from which battle the ship had emerged unscathed. There is no indication that he was legally qualified.

To put the trial of Ernest Leir in its historical context, the reader is reminded that at 0505 hrs on 21 March 1918 the German Army launched its final offensive in France, an offensive that, when it failed, would eventually bring the World War to a conclusion. The barrage that opened *Kaiserschlacht* employed about 4,000 field guns and over 6,000 pieces of other calibres of artillery. The barrage was hideously effective. It devastated the British front line, and the casualties were counted in the tens of thousands. The focus of the nation, in late March 1918, was firmly fixed on events in France, and against that backcloth the drama to be played out in HMS *Crescent*, merely concerning the loss of a submarine, pales almost into insignificance.

For Ernest Leir, however, it was of very great significance.

Capt Underhill opened by asking that the public be excluded from the proceedings, and the Court readily acceded to the request.[11] Effectively the trial was conducted 'in camera'.

Cdr Leir was asked first if he objected to the President or any member of the Court, and the record shows that he raised no such objection. Who knows, perhaps he viewed Hawksley as, literally, 'a friend at court'? The President of the Court Martial, and doubtless the senior of all the captains, was Capt William Slayter[12] of *Neptune*. Slayter was no stranger to courts martial; he had acted as prosecutor and had also filled the role of the accused.

The Court sat under the guidance of a Judge Advocate (JA), whose sole function was to rule and assist in matters of law. He played no part in making the professional judgements that were going to be needed when the thirteen nominated witnesses were examined. The name of the Judge Advocate is not given in this case, and that too is unusual.

All of the evidence at the trial was to be taken down in shorthand, and a typescript was produced by Chief Writer Thomas Patrick White. It is this document that makes up much of the bulk of the Admiralty file ADM 156–86 which is now open for public examination.

Much of the evidence would be a reiteration of that heard by the earlier Court of Inquiry, but this time the procedure would be crisper and the focus was purely on the judgement and actions of Cdr Leir and the loss of *K-17*. It is of passing interest that it was the loss of the boat and not the loss of the officers and men that formed the basis of the charge sheet. This is apparently because the crew of *K-17* were viewed as an integral part of the boat.

The court room consisted of a long table at which sat the nine members of the court, with the JA sitting at the President's side. To either side and in front of them were two tables. At one of these the Prosecuting Officer sat behind a veritable mountain of legal manuals and charts. At the other table there were two chairs, one for Leir and one for his 'Friend'. It is almost a service custom (and mere speculation on the author's part), but the probability is that all the tables were covered with grey issue blankets, and a White Ensign may have adorned the courtroom, providing a splash of colour (again idle speculation), but it is not speculation to say that a senior petty officer, who acted as court orderly, had a seat by the door. It was his function to summon witnesses and to carry out such minor tasks as the court required. The setting was formal, the atmosphere civil, but the tension was writ large on Leir's face. His ebullient personality was not to be seen as he set about defending his professional reputation and his career.

The first witness was the navigating officer of *Ithuriel*, Lt Denis Casey RNR. His evidence was unremarkable, although he told the court that when *Ithuriel* and her remaining submarines turned about, the turning circle was one mile and one cable.[13] He also said that when *Ithuriel* reversed her course she was closing the BCS at a combined speed of 37 knots. The President then asked, 'How long would two vessels, meeting at 37 knots with visibility of 2½ miles, see each other before they met?'

Either Casey had notice of the question or his mental arithmetic was very good or he was guessing, for he promptly replied, 'About 4½ minutes.'[14] Casey then went on to say that *Ithuriel* passed 2nd BCS at a distance of 4 cables on the starboard side but the destroyer screen on the port side. It does not take a great deal of imagination to see that, for all concerned, the manner that *Ithuriel* was threading west through a large formation that was heading east was potentially hazardous.

Lt J.G. Sutton, OOW of *Ithuriel*, followed Casey into the witness box and gave evidence as to course and speed. Initially that was N 89° E at 16 knots, but at 2012 hrs the course was altered to S 89° W under five degrees of helm.[15] Sutton estimated the turning circle at about 1½ miles.

Capt Underhill, the Prosecuting Officer, then asked Sutton, 'Did you anticipate any difficulty as a result of the sixteen-point turn, assuming that units or groups of the force were following?'

Sutton replied enigmatically, 'I do not wish to answer that question.'

The only conclusion one can draw from this answer is that Sutton did 'anticipate difficulty', and had disagreed with his Captain but was not going to say so in open court. Inexplicably, neither the Prosecution nor any member of the Court pressed the issue. Sutton then went on to say that *Ithuriel* had passed *Australia* to starboard and her destroyer screen, very close, to port. This was probably the very 'difficulty' that Sutton had anticipated. Capt Rowley-Conwy decided to put Sutton's role in the night's events into their proper perspective, and he cross examined the witness.

'What was your duty on the Bridge?'

'I was the Officer of the Watch, but the Captain and Navigating officer had taken over the ship.'

'You were not in charge of the ship?'

'No.'

Sutton was then questioned by the court, who clearly wanted to establish the degree of hazard facing his ship. Sutton responded by saying that *Ithuriel* had had to avoid the destroyers by altering course to starboard. However, he was vague about how many degrees of helm had been used: 'No, we were zig-zagging to avoid them. We came back on our own course again within two minutes. It was about one point.'

The remainder of Sutton's evidence was non-committal other than when he surmised that *K-17* had lost touch with the flotilla during the turn. However, he went on to say that when *K-17* could not be seen it was not reported to the Captain. This raises the question, 'Where was Leir at the time?' *Ithuriel* had an open bridge, it was noisy, a dark night, a stressing situation, and the OOW had charge of the ship. The ship was making a potentially hazardous passage, and in the normal course of events Leir would have been on the bridge, or, if absent, only for a few minutes. Again the matter was not pursued.

One can speculate about the relationship between Sutton and Leir before the trial, but afterwards it was unlikely to have been very warm.

Capt Arthur Bromley of *Courageous* confirmed that his ship was wearing the flag of the Vice-Admiral Light Cruiser Force (Evan-Thomas), but contributed only details of course and speed, which he said was 'N 74° E after May Island was abeam and speed 21 knots'. Bromley confirmed that the fleet following in his wake was expected to exit the Firth of Forth to the north of May Island by taking 'the Southern half of area ten, middle'.

The Court then enquired if 'a ship going on an opposite course and passing one of the forces would expect the remainder to be, roughly speaking, astern of the force which had passed?'

Bromley replied, 'Yes, I should think so.'[16]

'From your knowledge of the formation of the groups leaving the Firth of Forth and the general state of the weather as regards visibility, do you consider that it is a prudent course to turn back on units coming out?'

'Yes I think it is quite safe, one knows, more or less what course they are steering and I see no reason why they should not.'

Bromley's evidence, although he had been called by the Prosecution, was broadly favourable to Leir, as was the evidence of Capt Charles James Colebrooke Little of HMS *Fearless*, who now filled the recently vacated witness box. After the usual formalities to establish who Capt Little was and what his responsibilities were, he was asked, 'As leader of a flotilla is there any objection to K-class submarines proceeding to sea without their flotilla leader?'

'I do not think it would be advisable for the submarines to proceed to sea for the whole exercise without the services of a leader ... This is because the submarine of the senior officer is not suitably fitted for leading a unit of ships with the Fleet.'

'Would there be any objection to a flotilla leader temporarily leaving his submarines in charge of the senior officer with the idea of rejoining in a reasonable time?'

'I think that in a case of emergency, if the submarines had been furnished with their orders at the time, the orders for the exercise, there would be no objection from a point of view of safety.'

Little then confirmed that all submarines had a copy of the orders for Exercise EC1. He stated that his course, after May Island, was N 77° E and his speed was 21 knots. This course was to take him to the designated rendezvous with the Scapa force. The Prosecution now moved to the heart of the affair and asked for Little's account of the fatal collision with *K-17*:

I intercepted a signal at 1940 hrs concerning the collision between *K-14* and *K-22* and a further message at 2015 hrs saying that their position was to the northward of May Island. At that time I had passed May Island and I knew I was clear of it. In the region of 2030 hrs I was on the bridge and sighted two white lights fine on the port bow. I looked at these lights with my glasses and recognized the green lights on them almost a mile off. Two ships passed from port to starboard. I had on my own lights and in a very short space of time I sighted a third ship astern of the other two (*K-17*) but some distance astern of the second ship (*K-11*), probably half a mile at least. The two leading ships, in my judgement, were clearing, so my attention was centred on the third one, and it appeared to me to be quite a reasonable space of time I was watching her and waiting for her to alter course. But, she did not as far as I could tell and came straight towards me. Of course, I did not realize at the time we were on opposite courses and closing at such a rapid rate. A little time before the collision I ported to try to put the ship on a parallel course, but came into collision with her on her starboard side and the collision stopped the ship. I recognized her as *K-17* because she was different to all the others. The submarine swung round my port side, of course, it was quite dark and I thought she had gone straight down alongside of me, as a matter of fact she drifted slightly and sank a few minutes afterwards.

Capt Little, in answer to questioning, said that he had no knowledge that *Ithuriel* and the remnants of her flotilla were returning west back up the Firth of Forth. Probed by the Court, Little explained that he had been a flotilla leader for five or six years and that, in his experience, a submarine involved in a collision was particularly vulnerable because it had much less buoyancy than a surface ship. He advised that after such a collision the submarine's lights and wireless would probably be put out of action, and that was certainly the case with *K-17*. The Court then surmised that it would be more necessary for anybody to go to the assistance of two submarines in collision than if two destroyers had collided. Little confirmed that this was just the case, and in doing so he helped Leir's case.

Capt Underhill then asked a thrusting and important question of the witness, an officer who held a similar appointment to Leir. He enquired of Capt Little, 'Had you been in the position of the accused, would you yourself have turned back and gone to their assistance?'

Little recognized that by dint of his experience and his appointment his was critical evidence, because he was the submarine expert witness at this trial. His reply would be pivotal. The Captain paused, and then in carefully chosen words he replied,

> Taking all the circumstances of this particular case into account and the duties they were detailed for at the time I should have gone back to the submarines … The absence of any one particular unit was no great miss to the exercise … had I turned around I would have liked to have had my submarines with me.

'How long before you collided did you see the lights which you eventually found out to be *Ithuriel* and 13th Submarine Flotilla?'

'It was a very short space of time and I could not form any accurate estimate but, since the collision and taking the visibility at two and a half miles, I have ascertained that it would be about four minutes.'

Once again the Court probed gently and established that Capt Little had seen the lights of 13th SF, and switched on his navigation lights at full brilliancy. He opined that he had had two courses of action open to him: either to switch on his lights and stay on his course because the 'rule of the road' was in his favour, or else to keep his lights off and 'grope around as I liked in the dark'. He added that there was always the risk that in those circumstances 'some of his submarines of 12th SF would put their lights on, which would make an awkward situation.' A curious answer, for he then said that he issued an order to his flotilla, by lamp and also by wireless, to show lights.

The Court continued to worry the bone of the returning submarines and their value either at the scene of the collision or as a unit without its flotilla leader. Nevertheless, Charles Little stuck very firmly to his guns. He reiterated that the submarines would not have been effective without their leader, and in this specific case the leader could not have returned to them before later the following day. He did concede that the submarines would have been of little practical help at the scene of the collision. The suggestion that turning submarines at night was difficult was rejected, but he said that manoeuvring submarines was more akin to that of heavier ships than destroyers. The down side of Capt Little's evidence, as far as Leir was concerned, came right at the end, when he was asked by Capt Underhill, 'In the formation in which the units were, on leaving the Forth, would you have felt justified in turning back sixteen points until you had ascertained that the following units had been informed and the signal received by them?'

'I do not think I should have done it, but it is very difficult to speak after the event.'

Capt Charles Little had been a key witness, as he was the experienced commander of a submarine flotilla himself and, in this case, an expert witness if ever there was one. His evidence had been just slightly in Leir's favour, but the last remark had altered the balance.

Warrant Telegraphist E.W. Penny was called, but added little of importance and quickly disappeared from the stage, giving way to Cdr (N) W.E. Cornabe, the Navigating Officer of HMAS *Australia*. He testified to the very close encounter that his ship had had with 13th SF. He said that the last ship in the 13th SF line did not turn on navigation lights until 'she was practically abreast of the bow, too late for us to have made any alteration.' He commented that *Ithuriel* had passed about 1½ cables to starboard and the last submarine (*K-17*), only 'a matter of yards'. Cornabe said that he was aware of the standing orders for the disposition of a destroyer screen in poor visibility, and said that in this case the destroyers were in their screening positions and not astern.

The Captain of *K-11*, Cdr T.F.P. Calvert, was next to be called, and said that he was aware of the situation as he followed his leader. He was, however, phlegmatic when he gave his evidence, and said that when 2nd BCS was sighted he did not alter course, and passed the capital ships at a cable's distance. However, it was a different matter when it came to dodging the destroyer screen, and *K-11* made two severe course alterations before she was able to get back in station behind *Ithuriel*. She then passed *Fearless*, and looking astern, Calvert said he could see the lights of *K-17*.

Leir's Friend questioned Calvert closely, and Calvert admitted to misgivings about the course determined by his flotilla leader, but he agreed that with one formation (13th SF) with lights at full brilliancy and visibility between 2½ and 3 miles, the oncoming force (2nd BCS) should have been able to avoid any confrontation. The Defence, by questioning him, illustrated the difficulties experienced that night in communications between ships, and called Acting Warrant Telegraphist C.C. France, a senior member of the crew of *Ithuriel*. France produced the ship's signal log and was asked, 'Look at the log, what wireless and cypher signals were made by *Ithuriel* between 2000 hrs and 2120 hrs on the night of 31st January regarding her alteration of course?'

'The only cypher signal made is one timed at 2040. 'Priority. Submarine *K-12* and *K-22* have been in collision and are holed forward. I am proceeding to their assistance with 13th Submarine Flotilla. Position is 18 miles east magnetic from May Island.'[17]

'What is the time of origin?'

'The time the signal is handed in.'

'Can you explain then why the time of origin is 2040 and the signal was not dispatched until 2120?'

'In the first place this signal was brought down to be made in code shortly after 2000. I got the message coded and it was about to be sent when an additional message was brought down to be tacked onto it. Before I could get the message sent, the cypher officer, Lt Taylor, came down with another message and told me not to send the message that I had already got coded but to send the one he had brought down. He said, 'Don't send this one, it is coded and it ought to be in cypher.' He took both messages away to the bridge and brought me the one back in cypher.'

'At what time was it brought back to you in cypher?'

'I should say that it was between twenty minutes to and a quarter to nine because the stations had started transmitting.'

There was another brief exchange, and then: 'So we can take it that from the time the first message came down until the cypher message was ultimately got through was over an hour?'

'Yes.'

'Were any enquiries made from the bridge?'

'Yes, I informed them that the operator could not transmit it as the group stations were not transmitting.'

Clearly swift accurate communications were not the order of the day, and the time lag between the initiation of signals and their receipt was a factor in the 'Battle of the Isle of May'. No explanation was asked for or given to account for the twenty-minute or so gap between the origination of the signal and it being 'brought down.'

Cdr (N) J.D. Campbell of *Indomitable* and Cdr (N) K.E.L. Creighton of *New Zealand*, both expert navigating officers appointed to assist the court, were not examined by the Prosecution, but Capt Rowley-Conwy pursued them and the accuracy of the charts they had drawn up. Campbell, answering for both, agreed that the charts were in some measure a best estimate. The Defence asked, 'How close were the respective tracks of *Australia* and *Fearless*?' Campbell agreed that *Australia*'s track was about 450 yards north of that of *Fearless*, and this led to a brisk exchange on the veracity of the charts, as this particular track was not marked.

Conwy finally enquired, 'Could it be taken as a fair assumption that to accurately plot this, as now done, is, in absolute fact only a guess, and the data is unavailable for explaining this discrepancy?'

The answer, which did nothing to assist the Court, was, 'Yes, it is', and this reply closed the Prosecution case on a singularly low note.

The Defence could take some comfort in the absence of any condemnation being voiced by any witness appearing for the Prosecution. Mild concern at Leir's actions was about as strong as it had been. Cdr Ernest Leir was after all 'in command', and the Royal Navy was not a democracy then, nor is it today, nor should it ever be. Leir was paid to take decisions, was expected to do so, had done so and the only issue was, had he been negligent?[18]

As previously determined, the public benches in Court were empty as the proceedings were 'Secret', but somewhere in the fleet someone was running a book on the outcome of the trial. At this stage a betting man would have probably waged 'a bob or two' on Leir.

Cdr Leir had had ample time to prepare his defence. He was entitled to make an opening statement, and he was next to give evidence. He read the statement and then handed it in to the court. It is not a well-drafted document, and in places his argument is difficult to follow. This opening statement is reproduced here, in full, and in its original form:

I have been brought before this Court to answer the charge of negligently or by default causing the loss of *K-17*. I submit my actions may be separated into three different phases.

First. On receiving the signal the *K-22* and *K-12* had been in collision, was it essential to their safety and desirable for saving life that I should return to them as soon as possible?

Second. If this was so, was my 16 point turn in succession with small helm, lights at full brilliancy and my subsequent turn to Southward of 2 points to give more room, when I got my distance from Second Battlecruiser Squadron an unnecessarily dangerous manoeuvre?

Third. Immediately before collision, could I have done anything to avoid the collision?

With regard to the first point, should I have gone back? I would point out the extreme danger of a submarine collision which, of course, differs entirely from a collision of, say, two destroyers in so much that shock of collision is nearly certain to put their lights out and also to render their w/t useless and they are quite helpless.

This Court has heard the evidence of Captain Little with regard to this, and I submit to the Court that, not only was I justified in returning, but that had I not returned I would then have been greatly to blame – especially in view that the Fleet were going out for an exercise and not an exercise against the enemy.

My second point, if it is allowed that my decision to return was correct – was I guilty of any negligence or bad seamanship in my manoeuvre to do so? This appears to be a question only of visibility, especially as all squadrons were steering on approximately the opposite course and it required very little helm to avoid a collision. May Island light was visible for a distance of about ten miles and other navigation lights clearly visible for a distance of about three miles. When I was passing Second Battlecruiser Squadron at a distance of about two cables the ships were plainly seen, three battlecruisers being in sight at the same time without lights. My own navigation lights were on at full brilliancy and also those of the submarines astern of me. Their lights are brighter than ordinary navigation lights and no dimming switches are fitted. There was a slight mist in patches but, I did not consider it ever thick enough to prevent our lights being seen at a distance of two miles.[19]

When I got my distance from Second Battlecruiser Squadron I altered Southward two points which I considered was giving me plenty of room to pass other squadrons, and not sufficiently off the opposite course of the Fleet, so that only a small helm would be necessary to avoid them.

Before I turned I ordered a wireless to be made to *Barham* and *Courageous* that I was going back; this signal took a long time to code, the explanation of this has been produced in evidence. But, having given the order for it to be made I did not further think about it, until its usefulness as a warning for squadrons astern was of no value.

I regret the delay in the wireless signal not going through as quickly as I anticipated but, I would like to point out that even had it gone through and received by all units, the only difference that could have been made, if any, would be a slightly better look-out which was probably impossible.

There was no course signalled for the Fleet to steer from a position north of May Island. This, I am afraid, I did not sufficiently realize and the different courses that squadrons might be steering, instead of as usual all steering the same course exactly, which had they been doing, my course must have been perfectly safe.

The point 'A' mentioned in P. Z. Orders, for course to pass through could be steered for direct, which I considered all squadrons would do.

Captain of *Courageous* has stated in evidence that in his opinion the visibility was such that there was no danger incurred in my altering 16 points with such small helm and steering an opposite course to the Fleet with lights at full brilliancy. Evidence will be produced that the Rear Admiral of Second Battlecruiser Squadron considered the visibility was such that it was necessary to keep his destroyer screen out on their screening stations instead of dropping astern which would have been done had the weather been considered in any way thick or foggy. Therefore, this shows in his opinion visibility was such as to render his squadron liable to submarine attack.

The third point as to whether I could have done anything to prevent collision at the last moment I submit that myself and two officers were on the bridge, signal and look-out men, but in spite of a sharp look-out, regret *Fearless* was not seen by anyone, but *K-11*. The submarine astern of me saw her lights when close to which had apparently just been switched on.

I would point out that *Fearless* paint would make her harder to see when she was without lights.

Leir had made some valid points, but his convoluted phraseology did not make for clarity. He now had a less than stressing examination by his Friend. No doubt the questions and their answers were all well rehearsed, and this was really an opportunity to reinforce the bones of the earlier statement.

'Why did you not make a signal to the submarines astern of you to switch on navigation lights?'

'Because shortly after altering course I looked astern and counted three submarines by their lights I noticed they were all in good station.'

'Why did you show a yard-arm group in addition to the ordinary stern light?'

'It is my ordinary practice when altering course over four points at sea to show an additional stern light and as I had not got 'Z'[20] back for the alteration of sixteen points, to make certain that the submarines could not possibly miss me or miss my turn, I showed the yard-arm group.'

'What influenced you to bring the submarines back with you instead of leaving the senior officer of submarines in charge and proceed back by yourself?'

'I considered that there was no danger in my going back with the submarines, there was no necessity for them to go on except as an exercise, and I did not consider it a professional act to turn over to another officer a squadron which was out of station and had not a sufficient grasp of the situation to correct it.'

'What basis gave you the idea that by using three degrees of helm your tactical diameter would be in the vicinity of a mile?'

'In the course of exercising submarines at torpedo practice I have frequently used this helm and checked it.'

The accused having been bowled, in cricketing parlance, a series of easy full tosses on the leg side; the Prosecution took up the bowling, and this was bound to include some 'yorkers' and 'bouncers'.

'Do you consider that you would have had more freedom of action had you returned without your submarines?'

'No, after I had cleared the Second Battlecruiser Squadron I ordered them to return to harbour.'

'Were you aware that when you altered course sixteen points that the units astern of you had not received the signal?'

'Yes.'

'You were aware of that?

'Yes.'

'Did you consider the advisability of signalling, visually, that you had altered course ahead of you to the units that were coming in your track?'

'Yes I did, but I considered if I used the searchlight – the searchlight being probably the only method which would assist – that it would handicap the outgoing squadron by pointing my light to them as the searchlight is within a few feet of the bow light.'

'Were you aware that the course you were steering was not in the middle of the southern half of area ten middle?'

'I consider it is in the southern half of area ten middle.'

'And you thought that the units astern of you were steering the same course as you?'

'Yes within a degree or two.'

'Did it surprise you to find them as far south as you found them?'[21]

'Yes.'

'Did you actually order the submarines to return to harbour?'

'Yes.'

'You knew that the other submarine flotilla was ahead of you then?'

'I had expected it to be well on my starboard hand having passed *Australia* and altered two points to the southward.'

'But still ahead of you?'

'I ordered the submarine flotilla to return via south of May Island.'

'They had not actually parted company?'

'No.'

'At the same time they were probably not keeping station on you at the time of the collision?'

'I think the signal to return to harbour via May Island was made after the collision of *K-17* and *Fearless*. I was never at any time aware of this collision until I intercepted a wireless signal from *Fearless* and found she had collided.'

'You did not try to call up *Fearless* after passing Second Battlecruiser Squadron?'

'No.'

'What was the purport of the signal made in regard of the collision between *K-14* and *K-22*?'

'The first signal I received on the bridge at about 1945 was, "Nova Scotia. Both ships holed forward." '

'What did you hear subsequently?'

'Subsequent to that when the correct group had been found from the table which was not yet in force, it was made out to be, "From *K-22* to *Ithuriel* have been in collision with *K-12* both ships holed forward." '

'Did you judge from that, that there was a probability that both ships might sink very shortly?'

Yes, it is the exception rather than the rule for a submarine that has been in collision to float after it.'[22]

'At what time did you get the true version of the signal shown to you?'

'1955.'

'Then what was the next action you took after that?'

'I signalled the flotilla to alter course sixteen points to starboard.'

'At what time did you anticipate you would arrive at the spot of the collision?'

'I did not consider at what time I was going to arrive back, my first thought was to turn round and get there, and I went into the signal carefully and got its time of origin.'

'You did not know that first?'

'No, I did not look at it from that point of view; I simply read the signal, thought they required assistance and went on coming round to their assistance.'

'Then you had to make up your mind instantly as to whether you would take the submarines with you, or whether you would order them to go on under the leader[ship] of the senior officer?'

'Owing to the delay in correctly decoding the signal of distress received from the submarine, I was more anxious to get back than if there had been no delay, there was a delay of a quarter of an hour between the time of my getting the signal and it being sufficiently clear to me to act on; having lost a quarter of an hour, I was anxious to get back at once.'

'It would have involved delay in turning over the submarines to the next senior officer?'

'Yes, considerable delay.'

'What influenced you as to whether you would turn to port or starboard?'

'Before leaving harbour the area was altered from "North Middle" to "South Middle" and I knew that from an intercepted wireless signal an enemy submarine had been sighted in "North Middle" and I considered I should clear him when turning to starboard on the starboard course instead of to port.'

One more minor question brought Leir's evidence to a close, and it is surprising that the last answer recorded above was accepted without further interrogation. An enemy submarine had indeed been sighted at 1530 hours, and this had influenced Vice Adm Evan-Thomas as to the speed of his force. Leir's decision to turn was taken about four hours later, and it seems ingenuous in the extreme to presume that the enemy submarine would have remained stationary for that period of time, although her designated patrol area could have been fairly small. Nevertheless, she could have been anywhere in and around the mouth of the Firth. Given that the turning circle of the flotilla was about 2,200 yards, the difference in Leir's new course to starboard, proclaimed to be an anti-submarine track, is insignificantly different from a turn to port by 4,400 yards at most. Certainly it would not necessarily have avoided a hostile submarine patrolling to the east of the Isle of May.

Leir's part in the 'Battle of the Isle of May' was almost concluded, and his opening statement and then his cross examination had gone as well as could be expected. He now took his place alongside his Friend, and waited for the next witness, who was crucial to his case.

Lt W.H. Beedle, the OOW of *Fearless,* was called, and he acknowledged that he had seen the lights of *Ithuriel* and her submarines on his port bow. He added that visibility was about two miles. Having sighted the formation ahead, the lights of *Fearless* were switched on to full brilliancy. He was questioned further by the Prosecution.

'Did you make any remark to your captain about course being altered to avoid collision?'

'Yes.'

'What was that remark?'

'I asked the Captain if we would do anything to clear the stern of *K-17.'*

'Had the helm been altered then, shortly after the lights had been seen, how much helm would have been required to avoid collision? I mean to avoid the whole of the submarines astern of *Ithuriel* – would ten degrees of helm put on at the moment of sighting *Ithuriel?'*

'…Ten to fifteen degrees of starboard helm.'

Capt Underhill exercised his right, as the Prosecutor, to cross-examine Beedle, and when he had finished, the Court also sought clarification. Beedle confirmed that he saw the starboard and steaming lights of two ships about two miles ahead. He said that he saw a third ship immediately afterwards. These ships were crossing his bows from port to starboard but they were not in line because the third ship was well astern of the other two.

Lt Cdr P.A. Warre, flag lieutenant to the Rear Admiral Commanding the 2nd BCS, advised the court as to the disposition of the destroyer screen. He said that after the earlier warning the Admiral considered the squadron liable to submarine attack and made his dispositions accordingly.

Lt Cdr Warre was the final witness, and so at 1548 hrs on 25 March the courtroom was cleared and the Court retired to consider its finding. If a guilty verdict was determined the Court would return to hear pleas in mitigation of sentence and hear the service record of the accused. Then the Court would retire a second time to consider an appropriate sentence.

Leir was waiting. There was nothing he could do, and he was dependent on the judgement of his fellow officers. They were all practical, senior seamen with command experience. They would have had an appreciation of the nuances of the case before them and would have been aware of the peculiarities of the young submarine service, which had only been formed in 1901.

From its earliest days it was recognized that the submarine offered a very hazardous life style to its adherents. The first submarine lost to enemy action was HMS *E-3* on 18 October 1914, but in the ten years previously the Royal Navy, in a peacetime setting, had lost six boats to accidents and five to collisions. To be fair, this does not imply incompetence, because the submarine was an advancing technology and early mishaps and misjudgments were only to be expected.

By 1 February 1918 the picture had changed, and a further forty-two boats (including HMS *E-50*) had been lost, of which eight had been the result of a collision and six to assorted accidents.

Thus, of the fifty-three submarines that were sunk between March 1904 and 1 February 1918 only 57% were at the hands of the enemy. The loss of *K-1* and *K-17*, tragic and avoidable as it was, was, sadly, not particularly unusual.[23]

Notes

1. Secret File 453/H.F.1100
2. In this case' D' would have indicated 'I am not under command'.
3. The Beatty Papers 1989.
4. This is a reference to the six US battleships under the command of Rear Adm Hugh Rodman USN which were formed into the '6th Battle Squadron' and placed under the overall command of Beatty in late 1917. The six ships rotated in order to provide four on station at any one time. By June 1918 the squadron was fully integrated, and it took part in the surrender of the High Seas Fleet on 21 November 1918 in the Firth of Forth.
5. HMS *Opal* and *Narborough* were both lost when they ran ashore at South Ronaldsay on 12 January 1918. The weather was of extreme blizzard conditions. In all, 188 men were lost, and only AB William Sissons survived.
6. In December 1917 Jellicoe was abruptly dismissed from the post of First Sea Lord by Sir Eric Geddes, the First Lord of the Admiralty. This would have been with the agreement of the Prime Minister, David Lloyd George.
7. The Beatty Papers 1989

8. Rear Adm Sir William Packenham, who had followed Beatty in command of the Battlecruiser Fleet in December 1916. He was promoted vice admiral in 1918 and died in 1933, aged 72.

9. Beatty's movement up the promotion ladder, at least in part, would have been due to the patronage of Fisher. Clearly, any gratitude Beatty might ever have felt had evaporated by 1918.

10. A Welshman, Rowley-Conwy was 43 at the time of the trial, and a relatively junior captain, having been promoted to that rank only in December 1916. He had spent most of his service in destroyers and had won several commendations for his efficiency.

11. A court martial has the same status as any other British court in respect of public access. The exclusion of the public on this occasion can be readily understood given the sensitivity of the case and the deleterious effect on national morale that airing the facts could cause. This is similar to the arrangements at the *Oceanic* investigation.

12. This is the same Capt Slayter who had faced trial by court martial over the stranding and eventual loss of RMS *Oceanic* in September 1914. He had been promoted to captain in 1907 and was now aged 47.

13. This was a distance of 2,200 yards.

14. In fact '4 minutes' would have been more accurate.

15. A standard helm is 15°, and it begs the question as to whether this slow turn was because the K boats were so cumbersome.

16. This answer did not make allowance for the spread of the destroyer screen of the capital ships. The track of the force moving east to the sea was, of necessity, far more than one ship's width. Therein is the difficulty of Lt Sutton.

17. *Ithuriel* had altered course with her flotilla to S 89° W, and if this position was correct she was now steering directly at the Isle of May.

18. The Imperial Dictionary (1878) definition of negligent is 'Careless; heedless; apt or accustomed to omit what ought to be done'.

19. The closing speed was 37 knots, and the two miles would have been covered in 3½ minutes.

20. The acknowledgement of a signal.

21. This rather obscure question presumably refers to the 12th SF and 5th BS.

22. In this specific case, *K-6*, *K-14* and *K-22* all returned safely to harbour.

23. To bring these statistics up to date: The Royal Navy has suffered 167 casualties in its submarine fleet, of which 116 were the direct result of contact with the enemy. A remarkably high proportion, 38, or 30%, of these have been attributed to contact with mines – a particularly lethal form of collision, and one that gives a submarine little or no chance of long-term survival.

CHAPTER SIX

The Verdict – Who was Really to Blame?

There was the sound of heavy boots, followed by a sharp knock on the wardroom door. When the door was opened, the court orderly, a three-badge petty officer, was standing in the wardroom flat. He said in studied, neutral tones, 'They are ready for you now, Sir.' Leir stood and exchanged a grimace with his Friend. Together they made their way back into the courtroom, where the President, Capt W.F. Slayter, the Captain of HMS *Neptune*, would soon pronounce on finding and possibly on sentence.

Leir entered the courtroom and saw that all the members of the Court were now wearing their hats. It was an indication of the gravity of the moment. Leir gave a gasp; his Friend gripped his arm. The gasp had been one of relief because the hilt of Ernest Leir's sword was towards him. Leir and Rowley Conwy stood to attention. Both knew that there was not a lot to say. The Judge Advocate nodded his bewigged head to the President; Capt William Slayter picked up the cue, cleared his throat and said crisply, 'Commander Ernest William Leir, the charge against you, "being a person subject to the Naval Discipline Act, that you did, on the thirty-first day of January 1918 negligently or by default suffer His Majesty's Submarine *K-17* to be lost" is not proved[1] and you are acquitted.'

It was as simple and as quick as that. The tension in the room evaporated immediately, and there were smiles on the faces of many of the Court, all of whom recognized that 'there but for the grace of God go I'.

Leir's hand was shaken by most of those present. He clipped his sword back on to his sword-belt over his left hip, knowing he was now free to resume his command and play his part in winning the war. But first there were drinks to be taken in *Ithuriel*'s wardroom. Several drinks, probably.

Ernest Leir was one of nineteen officers who faced trial by court martial in the period 1 February to 22 March 1918.[2] This group of accused officers faced an amazing array of charges, including, among others, drunkenness, embezzlement, wilful disobedience and neglect of duty. Some of those who went to trial were clearly an absolute disgrace to the Service, and their offences were broadly of dishonesty or un-officer-like behaviour. Of the nineteen, Leir

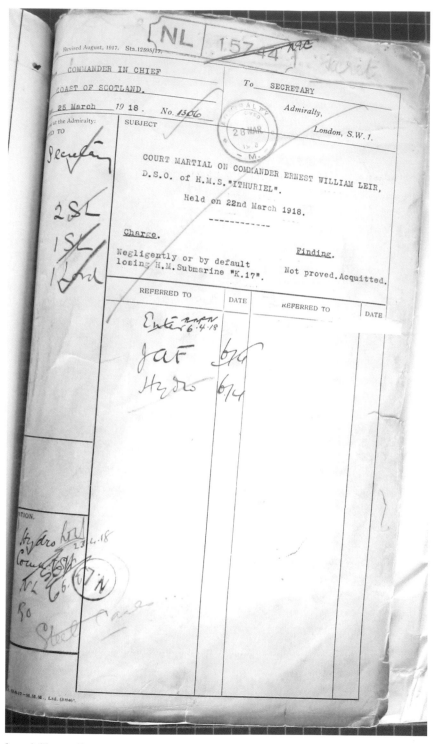

The closed file on Commander Ernest William Leir. *(Jeff Birch)*

was one of only three to be acquitted, and of course his honour had never been in question. Nevertheless, well might he have celebrated with a glass or two!

On 6 April 1918 Mr G.W. Ricketts, acting on behalf of Mr R.B.D. Acland, the Judge Advocate of the Fleet, confirmed that the charge had been in order and that the conduct of the court had been 'regular'.

After the promulgation of the verdict there was a predictable exchange of correspondence from Scapa Flow to the Admiralty and back to Rosyth. The Hydrographer of the Navy also offered a view. This latter, an expert on all matters navigational, summed up admirably on 8 April and in a loose minute on the file.[3] He said,

The acquitted Commander Leir photographed much earlier, in about 1912. *(Leir Family)*

Ithuriel appears to have passed May Island at a greater distance than *Fearless* did, and in addition was steering five degrees more to the northward than the latter, see chart prepared by the navigating officers. The result was that her turning circle, although large, did not take her clear of *Fearless* track and the alterations of two points to port after passing *Australia* made her cross the track at an angle of 27 degrees from port to starboard of *Fearless*.

Fearless saw *Ithuriel* and submarines crossing, but kept her course in compliance with the rule of the road, altering course to starboard at the last to try to avoid collision with *K-17*. There is no evidence as to what the latter did, but she should have ported and passed *Fearless* port to port.

Under all the circumstances the finding of the court is concurred in, though it is considered that Commander Leir would have been better advised had he kept as far southward as possible from the time he made the alteration of course to return.

The file was closed. It would remain closed and gathering dust until 1994. Leir had been acquitted. Nevertheless, 104 men were still dead after a series of avoidable collisions, and surely someone, somewhere, was responsible. Who should shoulder the blame for the debâcle?

There are several candidates.

The captains of *K-22*, *K-17* and *Fearless* are all possibilities, but what of Vice Adm Sir Hugh Evan-Thomas? The large Rosyth force sailed at his direction, and this deployment was unusual, if only because of the size of the force and its diversity. Evan-Thomas had over forty ships under his command, but the juxtaposition of the various components of that force had been specified earlier in the exercise order signed by Adm Beatty. Evan-Thomas then took local decisions, for example reacting to the submarine sighted five miles south-east of the Isle of May on the afternoon of 31 January and before the Rosyth force sailed. The degree to which the various squadrons and flotillas had had opportunities to practise that which Vice Adm Evan-Thomas expected of them on 31 January is not known, and at ninety years' distance the facts are obscured by the legendary 'mists of time'. Adm Beatty had a view on this issue and had been swift to judgement; in a letter to his wife he had commented on 'the lack of sea experience' (see page 89) as a cause of the disaster.

If this was indeed the case, then both Beatty and Evan-Thomas bear the responsibility for not preparing their ships better. Despite this lack of sea experience the exercise order presented the short voyage to the North Sea as purely routine, and for individual ships so it was. For a squadron or flotilla it should have been SOP (standard operating procedure). It is the combination of the various components that makes the deployment noteworthy.

It was on the direct orders of Adm Beatty that the 12th and 13th SFs were grouped in the middle of his formation, where they would be most vulnerable to the series of mishaps that then occurred. Evan-Thomas concurred with this decision, and as the admiral in command of the Rosyth force he has to take ownership of what followed. His departure plan made no allowance for anything to go wrong. In circumstances that combined sailing in darkness, reduced visibility, high speed, a large number and disparity of vessels and the inevitability of imprecise navigation and station keeping, the chances of mishap were not inconsiderable. The Admiral's orders make no mention of the burning of navigation lights because lights, in all their forms, were a constant topic at both the Court of Inquiry and at Leir's Court Martial. Evan-Thomas's acceptance of Beatty's orders in combination with his own served to put all the ingredients for an accident or series of accidents firmly in place just as soon as the exercise order had been promulgated.

It is a commander's responsibility to foresee anything in his plan which could go awry, and to take steps to eliminate the risk, or at the very least minimize that risk. The evidence is that, in this respect, Evan-Thomas failed. A study of the personal file of Evan-Thomas makes reference to his being the subject of censure for the collision between HMS *Warspite* and *Valiant* on 24 August 1916. The Board of Inquiry concluded that, 'He failed to exercise the necessary control in making arrangements before the movement of ships at night.'[4]

The 'Battle of the Isle of May' was at night, and Evan-Thomas had clearly not learned his lesson. Given his track record for having insufficient control over

Admiral Sir Hugh Evan-Thomas GCB KCMG MVO. Photographed in 1921 when he was Commander-in-Chief the Nore. (*National Portrait Gallery*)

his ships at night, he was fortunate not to have been called to account. The pragmatic view is that, if bringing admirals to trial was a favoured option it would be a much more common occurrence, but at that level there are political considerations to be weighed. The reality is that a more junior officer had to be called to book.

The Court of Inquiry and the later trial of Ernest Leir both had a narrow focus; as a result the departure plan was never subject to a critical professional examination.

The breakdown in communications between the staff of Vice Adm Evan-Thomas and the authority responsible for policing the anti-submarine barriers was a major factor. Had correct communications been established, then the 'unknown small vessels' might have been more aware of the movement of a large body of ships, and would have stood clear. Are the inadequate communications and the ineffective liaison between Evan-Thomas and those responsible for the security of the mouth of the Firth yet another example of Adm Evan-Thomas having insufficient control?

Evan-Thomas had issued orders that at the time were, apparently, perfectly acceptable to all concerned, and certainly there is no record of any dispute or even reservations. He led the force from Rosyth and was well out into the North Sea before any of the collisions occurred. Realistically, he could not anticipate a series of events that took place miles behind him and which he could not influence.

It would be unreasonable to lay the direct responsibility for the 'Battle of the Isle of May' at the door of Evan-Thomas, but it would not have taken place if he had been more diligent.

The sea-going officers had, for the most part, acquitted themselves very well. Cdr Thomas Harbottle in *K-14* had responded to the unexpected sight of the two small vessels in an appropriately professional manner. He steered his boat out of danger, and in the normal course of events would have resumed his station as a matter of complete routine if his helm had not jammed. The jammed helm served to take him well to port of his previous track, and he had every reason to suppose that he was well out of danger from any following vessel. His boat was not under command, and it is unreasonable to blame him for the first collision with *K-22*.

Lt Cdr Charles de Burgh, commanding *K-22*, was well off track, and it was cruel misfortune that brought his boat into collision with *K-14*. This one simple and avoidable incident was the trigger for all that followed. The fact is that if *K-22* had maintained her correct station and not lost sight of the boat ahead (*K-12*) she would never have been close enough to hazard *K-14*, let alone hit her and kill two men.

On this basis, de Burgh's poor seamanship makes him culpable, and he bears great responsibility for initiating the loss of two boats and 104 lives. The court of inquiry had curiously and inexplicably absolved him in this instance, but initially and perversely blamed him for the later collision with *Inflexible*. Rear Adm Goodenough and his Court of Inquiry failed to attribute blame to de Burgh, which is not the least of their failings.

At both the Court of Inquiry and at the Court Martial, the actions of *K-17* and her Captain, Lt Cdr Henry John Hearn, were not examined. Perhaps it was a matter of not speaking ill of the dead. However, there can be no dispute that, after Leir turned his flotilla around, *K-17* fell out of station and was significantly astern of *K-11*. This had the knock-on effect of putting *K-12*, the last in line, also out of station. Notwithstanding the hazard inherent in the course selected by his flotilla leader, Lt Cdr Hearn was a capable officer and he had known the rule of the road since boyhood.

Hearn would most certainly have been on the bridge and fully in command of *K-17* in her journey westwards up the Firth. This was undoubtedly a hazardous passage, and charge of the boat would not have been delegated to one of the other officers. The decision not to alter course was Hearn's alone.

Cdr Leir ordered the course to be sailed by the 13th SF, and when *K-17* following that prescribed track saw that she would cross the bows of *Fearless*, it should have been evident to her Captain, Lt Cdr Hearn, that his overriding responsibility remained the safety of his boat and his crew – he had no moral responsibility to follow a track that would needlessly put either at risk. The obvious decision to turn to starboard and pass *Fearless* port to port should have been no more than day-to-day routine. As it was, Hearn held his track, and doing so cost him his life, those of his men and his boat. Had he survived he must surely have faced trial for this incompetent ship handling. His responsibility by far outweighs that of de Burgh in that his boat was sunk and he and forty-six of his men were killed.

Capt Charles Little, commanding *Fearless* and the 12th SF, in the circumstances did what his training dictated. As an experienced submariner himself he would have been painfully aware of the limitations of the K-class boats. He should have realized that if *K-17* was going to alter course to avoid him then she would have had to do so soon after she sighted *Fearless*, given that their combined closing speed was well in excess of 30 knots. However, it is mandatory for a 'right-of-way vessel' to maintain her course and speed until it becomes clear that the 'give-way vessel' cannot avoid a collision by her own manoeuvre alone. In this respect Little was faultless, and although the likelihood of a collision was identified on the bridge of *Fearless* some short time before the clash, Capt Little had no case to answer. Reducing his speed might just have helped, but in those crowded waters it might also have made a difficult situation worse.

If there is a single culprit, the search must be widened, and perhaps the search should go back to a time well before the 'Battle of the Isle of May'. In January 1915 the failure of the J-class boats to meet their specification and provide a surface speed of 21 knots is the start point.

Admiral of the Fleet Sir John Fisher was adamant in his need for 'fleet' submarines, and his intransigence is covered earlier in this book. He created the K-class submarine that history now tells us is the maritime equivalent of the Ford Edsel.[5] The men who crewed the boats hated them, and their record of mechanical and often other inexplicable failures sapped the confidence of all of those who were associated with the class. The courage of the men who sailed in these inadequate vessels is remarkable. On 31 January 1918 it was the inexplicable jamming of the helm of *K-14* that was the trigger for all the events that followed in the proximity of the Isle of May. It led, inexorably, to the collision with *K-22*, the return of *Ithuriel* and the 13th SF, and, in turn, to the ramming and sinking of *K-17* and *K-4*.

The K boat was the brainchild and creation of Jackie Fisher. He would have readily savoured any successes enjoyed by the class, but there were none. The converse is true, and the record is one of unremitting failure. On that basis is it fair to place on the shoulders of Admiral of the Fleet Baron Kilverstone GCB OM GCVO responsibility for the failure of the K class in general and, as such, for the single, inexplicable failure in *K-14* that led directly to the 'Battle of the Isle of May' in particular?

Of course it is not.

Fisher did not design the boats, but he caused them to be designed. He hastened them into service, it has to be said, with the help of fawning subordinates, and there is no record of any of Their Lordships opposing the introduction of this class of submarine into the fleet.

Those responsible for the mayhem off the Isle of May are a disparate group. The part played by the Director of Naval Construction and his apparent uncritical support of Fisher should not be discounted. Fisher, of course, has a case to answer, but so have the designers at Vickers, the admirals who acquiesced at their construction, the officers who accepted the first boats at their trials and the overriding bureaucracy that made it easier to take the class into service than to scrap them. That bureaucracy persisted in maintaining K boats in some form or another until well after the war, by which time their *raison d'être* had long since disappeared. Better, perhaps, to let Jackie Fisher rest on his well-deserved laurels.

Finally, what of Cdr Ernest William Leir? His decision to reverse his course and to steam back up the Firth of Forth into the face of several squadrons of fast-moving ships was examined by nine captains of the Royal Navy. They were all very experienced seamen. They understood all the issues of wind, tide, visibility, ship handling communication and, above all else, the responsibility that comes with command. This sage group tried Leir and found the case against him 'not proved'. From a layman there is admiration for the moral strength of Leir's decision and amazement that he was entirely exonerated.

The 'Battle of the Isle of May' was never a 'battle', but it was a series of avoidable accidents – accidents that singly and in isolation would have been relatively unremarkable. It is their very combination in such a short time frame that will, for ever, group them together.

The remains of *K-4* and *K-17* lie in 155 feet of very cold, clear water about 1½ miles north-east of the Isle of May. *K-4* is in two very distinct pieces but *K-17* is still intact. It is reported that, although her conning tower is bent over and broken open, cups and dinner plates, still neatly stacked, can readily be seen. Today, divers sometimes visit the two wrecks, which are quite correctly respected as war graves.

It is now ninety years that have passed. The families who knew and loved the 104 brave and trusting men who died here have themselves passed on, and the events of January 1918 are now no more than sad footnotes to history.

The memorials to those who died are to be found in St Mary Patten Church, Eastcheap, London,[6] at Anstruther in Fife, at the Royal Navy Submarine Museum at Gosport, on various war memorials and finally in this book, in which I set out to tell the full story.

Postscript

Just as men have their life span, so too have ships, and the five ships that played a part here – HMS *Courageous, Ithuriel, Fearless, Venetia* and *Inflexible* – all served on after the 'Battle'.

Courageous was one of the most long lived. She had only a minor role in January 1918, and after peace was declared in November 1918 she was, in effect, redundant. Her design as a battlecruiser was by now recognized as making her very vulnerable. A decision was taken in 1924 to convert her to an aircraft carrier, a process that took four years and cost about £90 million at 2008 prices. She was no less vulnerable, however, and on 17 September 1939, with World War II only two weeks old, she fell victim to *U-29* south-west of Ireland. Having been torpedoed, she sank in about fifteen minutes. A total of 518 officers and men went down with her. It was the beginning of the end of the original battlecruisers, and in the ensuing conflict three came to a sticky end. The most famous of the class was 'the Mighty Hood'. Her lack of armour and instantaneous fiery end have been the subject of great debate ever since. *Repulse* was sunk from the air by the Japanese; *Glorious* was converted to an aircraft carrier and was lost serving in that role; *Furious* was also converted, but she survived; *Renown* also saw the war to its end.

Ithuriel's life was short. She was launched in 1916 and had her brief moment in the spotlight at the Isle of May. In 1919 Ernest Leir relinquished command of the ship and moved on. *Ithuriel* was earmarked for disposal, and in 1921 she was scrapped. With a degree of irony, she was broken up in Germany.

Fearless had a short life, too. She was launched in 1913, and in 1921 she was sold for scrap as the Royal Navy reshaped itself for the peace. Her name has lived on, and her successors achieved fame, not least in the Falklands war.

Venetia was one of a very large class of twenty-five destroyers, many of which gave sterling service in the Second World War. The last two of the class were *Versatile* and *Vendetta*, both of which remained in service until the summer of

Admiralty V & W-class destroyer, HMS *Venetia*.

1948. *Venetia* did not survive World War II, and she was mined and sunk off Margate in October 1940.

Inflexible was present when the German High Seas Fleet surrendered at the mouth of the Firth of Forth in November 1918, and she escorted the rusted and mutinous German ships to anchor. In 1919, she was paid off to the Reserve Fleet. She was offered for sale to Chile in 1920, but the purchase was not completed, and in 1922 she was sold. She was broken up in 1923 – in Germany.

As for the K-class submarines, their individual fates are briefly summarized in Appendix 1.

Notes

1. The design of a submarine, particularly in her earlier form, provided severely limited visibility from a platform that was relatively low in the water and often below the water. The involvement of submarines in collisions, usually with surface vessels, is almost to be expected.
2. The verdict 'Not proved' is not to be confused with the Scottish verdict 'Not proven'. 'Not proved', unsatisfactory as it is, was nevertheless the nomenclature used at the time.
3. Return of officers tried by court martial during the quarter ended 31 March 1918 (HM Stationery Office).
4. ADM 156–86.
5. N42/4390 of 28/4/16 refers.
6. The Ford Edsel was produced between 1956 and 1960. It was a design and marketing failure on a gigantic scale for the Ford Motor Company, which managed to get just about everything wrong. It was a self-inflicted wound, and someone said of the car, 'The aim was right but the target moved.'

CHAPTER SEVEN

Whatever Happened to …?

T he participants who had a role at the battle and its aftermath all survived World War I. Those who served in World War II came through that as well, and most lived on into comfortable old age and died peacefully in their beds. One participant, Lt Richard Sandford, died young, but his name is never likely to be forgotten, as this chapter reveals.

Vice-Admiral Sir Hugh Evan-Thomas GCB KCMG MVO
Commander, the Rosyth force

Evan-Thomas was born in 1862. There is no doubt that his reputation as made at Jutland when he was Rear Admiral commanding the 5th BS. Following that battle, honours were showered upon him and he was decorated by the Russians, French, Italians and Japanese. He was promoted vice-admiral in September 1917.

Exercise EC1 was the first and only chance he had to command such a large force, and after the exercise he moved his flag back to *Barham*, finishing the war still in command of the 5th BS. In 1919 he was appointed KCMG and in 1920 was promoted to admiral and made Commander-in-Chief, the Nore. This was his final appointment, and he retired in 1924 to Charlton, a village near Shaftesbury.

His retirement was short lived, and he died, aged 66, in 1928. His flagship HMS *Barham* outlived him, but was sunk with heavy loss of life when she was torpedoed in 1941.

Captain William Frith Slayter
President of the Court Martial

Slayter's stranding of *Oceanic* certainly limited his career, and towards the end of the war, in September 1918, and still a captain, Admiral Beatty recommended him for consideration for flag rank. Despite this Their Lordships earmarked him for an administrative appointment, and he was appointed as Captain, HM Dockyard, Rosyth. However, in January 1919 he was promoted to rear admiral, and in the *London Gazette* (*LG*) of 16 September 1919 notification appeared of his appointment as Commander of the Bath (CB). This was in recognition for the 'excellence of his work at Rosyth'. The honours system is usually quite a slow-moving process (other than in the case of some gallantry awards), and CB is usually awarded on the completion of an appointment. Slayter's decoration was given with unusual haste after only a few months in the job. One wonders why.

He retired in April 1921 in the rank of rear admiral, and was promoted to vice-admiral on the retired list in July 1924.[1] Further promotion to admiral followed in February 1928. He died in May 1936, aged 69.

Rear Admiral William Edmund Goodenough CB MVO
President of the Court of Inquiry

Goodenough was born in 1867, and he joined the Navy in 1882. He had a distinguished career and fought in the three of the major actions in World War I. He excelled at the battles of both Dogger Bank in August 1914 and later that year Heligoland Bight. At Jutland, on 31 May 1916, he had commanded the 2nd Light Cruiser Squadron, and on that day he flew his pennant in HMS *Southampton* and had under command *Birmingham*, *Nottingham* and *Dublin*. The performance of the squadron drew plaudits, and he was promoted to rear admiral and given command of a battlecruiser squadron, a post he held until the end of the war.

His inept handling of the Court of Inquiry in February 1918 drew no public criticism, but as that inquiry was conducted in secret, it was unlikely to do so. Without doubt Goodenough failed the officers and men lost at the 'Battle of the Isle of May' by not examining in appropriate detail the root causes of their deaths. He should have reviewed the Vice-Admiral's exercise planning, and in particular his lack of co-ordination with the boom defence organization. Had he done so he might have reached the same conclusions as the author.

It would have limited his future advancement if he had called Evan-Thomas, his senior officer, to give evidence. To be fair, it would have taken enormous moral courage, would have put Goodenough's career on the line and might well still have achieved nothing. To be fair to Goodenough, if a similar set of circumstances occurred today it's possible that there would be much the same result.

Goodenough not only conducted an inadequate investigation but his unbalanced attribution of blame further compounded his mistakes. The conclusion to be drawn is that Goodenough failed in his duty.

Goodenough sailed on. He received the *Croix de Guerre* and then he moved to be,

Admiral Sir William Goodenough, pictured in later life.

briefly, the Superintendent of Chatham Dockyard. In 1920 he was appointed Commander-in-Chief, Africa Station, and promoted to vice-admiral. A KCB followed. In 1923 he was given command of the Reserve Fleet, and in 1924 was made Commander-in-Chief, the Nore (in succession to Adm Sir Hugh Evan-Thomas). He was promoted to admiral in May 1925 and advanced to GCB. From 1929 and until he retired in 1930 William Goodenough was 1st and Principal Naval ADC to HM The King. He assumed the presidency of the Royal Geographic Society in 1930, a post he held until 1933. William Goodenough retired in May 1930, and on the outbreak of the Second World War he offered his services, 'in any capacity'.[2] His offer was not taken up, almost certainly because, at his age and seniority, it would have been difficult to find him a post. He died in January 1945, aged 78.

Commander Thomas Cecil Benfield Harbottle
Captain of HM Submarine K-14

Harbottle, who was born in 1885, continued in command of *K-14* for only three weeks after its collision with *K-22*. He was then moved to command of *L-9*, and in August 1919 he was given command of the 4th SF.

It was in December 1919 that he faced a court martial, charged with (1) 'Negligently or by default hazarding *H-41*', (2) 'Negligently performing the duty imposed upon him in not taking the necessary measures to insure the safety of the submarines lying alongside his ship'. In the first case the charge was 'Not proved'. The second charge was 'Proved', and Cdr Harbottle was reprimanded. He completed his appointment but thereafter his career stalled. In 1923 he applied for transfer to the naval wing of the RAF. It was noted at the time that, 'He cannot hold out any hope in this connection.' He promptly retired at the age of 38, but re-enlisted in 1925.

He was promoted captain in 1930. Thereafter he held a number of posts in the Naval Ordnance Inspectorate, and finally retired in September 1944.

Lieutenant-Commander Samuel Maryon Gorlon Gravener
Captain of HM Submarine K-7

Gravener continued in command of *K-7* until November 1919, and he was then appointed to HMS *Inconstant*. This was only until April of the following year, when he asked to be relieved as he suffered from chronic sea sickness.[3] In 1920 he was appointed as executive officer of a large surface ship, but he found the transition from submarines difficult, and he was found sufficiently wanting for the report written upon him by Capt Lewis to be damning. Perhaps the most crushing judgment of him was that the Captain concluded, 'He has no sense of humour'. Notwithstanding the poor report, very curiously and inconsistently Lewis still recommended Gravener for promotion. His career marked time from that point, and he was given command of HMS *Diligence*. The ship was 'in reserve', and so Gravener had no chance to impress and recover his fortunes.

He was placed on the retired list at his own request in 1926 with the rank of commander. He joined the Royal Observer Corps in 1938 but returned to the Royal Navy in 1940, and served throughout the war until he was released in September 1945 at the age of 59.

Captain Rafe Grenville Rowley-Conwy
The accused's Friend

Rowley-Conwy was decorated with the CMG in 1919 for his services as Captain (D) of a flotilla. He went on to Command HMS *Caledon* as flag captain to Rear Adm Wilmot. He retired from the service in 1922.

In 1935 he became HM Lord Lieutenant in the county of Flint, where he had been born in 1875, and held this post until his death in April 1951, aged 76. His service record does not show any further promotion on the retired list, and one wonders why. Nevertheless, the archive of the Lord Lieutenancy of Flint lists him as 'Rear Admiral'.

He volunteered for service in 1940 and was employed as a commodore RNR on convoys. He reverted to the retired list in 1942.

Commander Charles de Burgh DSO
Captain of HM Submarine K-22

Charles de Burgh was another of the 1898–1900-vintage *Britannia* group who became effective submariners. He had been employed in the submarine service since September 1909; *K-22* was his sixth boat and his fourth command. In July 1917, while in *G-8*, he successfully torpedoed an enemy submarine, and his award of the DSO was announced in November 1917.

He was obviously a very physical officer, because his record speaks of his enthusiasm for games. It also comments more than once on his 'casual attitude'. He relinquished command of *K-22* in mid-February 1918, and assumed command of *K-16*. He came to the attention of Their Lordships of the Admiralty when, in May 1920, he allowed the submarine *L-17*, under his command, to collide with a floating dock in Haslar Creek. He remained in command of submarines until 1928, when he was appointed Commander (S) of the 6th SF. Thereafter he languished in the rank of commander in a series of low-key appointments. He opted to retire in July 1932, aged 46.

He was accorded the rank of captain on retirement, and was recalled in 1939. He served throughout the war as 'Naval officer in control of shipping and convoys'. He was finally discharged in January 1946, aged 60.

Captain Charles James Colebrooke Little
Captain of HMS Fearless

Charles Little had already commanded six submarines (*H-4*, *A-7*, *B-7*, *C-5*, *C-10*, *D-1*) before he was appointed to command the 12th SF, and so he was a vastly experienced submariner. He relinquished command of his flotilla in 1918 and was appointed CB (Civil) for his performance in that command. He went on to command HMS *Cleopatra* in the Baltic, and, most unusually, he was appointed CB (Military)[4] on his completion of that appointment. He was Director, Trade Division of the Naval Staff, for two years until 1922, and in between times was a member of the British delegation to the Washington Naval Conference in 1921. He attracted plaudits for his significant contribution to this conference.

He served in the Mediterranean from 1923 to 1924, and went on to command HMS *Iron Duke* for two years from 1926. He was now on his way up, and that was evidenced by his appointment as Director of the Royal Naval Staff College, Greenwich.

In 1930, at the age of 50, he was promoted rear admiral, and went to command the 2nd BCS. He reverted to submarines in 1931 as Head of the Submarine Service. The year 1932 saw him as a Lord Commissioner of Admiralty and the Deputy Chief of Naval Staff. He was promoted to vice-admiral in 1933 and given command of the China station in 1936. While in that job he was promoted to admiral. The outbreak of war found Charles Little as Chief of Naval Personnel, but in 1941 he went off to the USA to head a Joint Staff Mission. He returned to the UK in 1942 to be Commander-in-Chief, Portsmouth. He was filling this appointment when the war ended in 1945. He was awarded the Legion of Honour (USA) for his services during Operation Overlord. In 1945 he handed over as Commander-in-Chief to a man called Layton – who at one time had commanded *K-6* and had been his subordinate in the 13th SF, some twenty-seven years earlier.

Later in 1945 Adm Sir Charles Little GCB GBE retired from the Navy, aged 65. He enjoyed a very long retirement and died in June 1973, aged 93.

Commander Geoffrey Layton
Captain of HM Submarine K-6

The Court of Inquiry attributed any blame arising from the collision of *K-6* with *K-4* to Lt Richard Sandford, and Layton was unaffected other than by the loss of so many of his friends.

Later in 1918, and after the 'Battle of the Isle of May', and for 'Other services', Layton was awarded the DSO. He was a man to watch and, as they say in the services, 'His card was marked accordingly.' He was promoted to captain in 1922 and given command of the 2nd SF, and later, command of the 1st SF.

In the two years between 1927 and 1929 he served as 'Deputy Director of Operations' at the Admiralty – the type of appointment only given to officers with the potential to rise to the highest levels. He was selected to attend the Imperial Defence College in 1930, and on completion of the course he was sent to the China station to be chief of staff to the admiral in command.

A brief time in command of the battlecruiser HMS *Renown* was followed by two years at home in Portsmouth in an administrative shore job. In 1935 he was selected for promotion to rear admiral, and when he put up his new gold braid in 1936 he returned to the Admiralty, this time as Director, Personnel Services – a plum job for a high-grade official. He was appointed CB in 1936.

Storm clouds were now gathering, and in 1938 he took command of the Battlecruiser Squadron. War duly broke out, and in 1940 Layton, as a vice-admiral, was sent back to China as Commander-in-Chief of the China station. The war in the East went very badly, and after Adm Phillips lost his two capital ships off the coast of Malaya, and Singapore fell, Layton moved his headquarters to Ceylon (now Sri Lanka). He was given command of all military forces on the island, and of the civilian infrastructure too. He was promoted KCB in 1940.

Admiral Sir Geoffrey Layton in 1945.

He prepared Ceylon for a Japanese attack to such effect that, when the predicted air assault took place, it was repulsed with heavy Japanese losses and they did not try again. Layton played an important part in making Ceylon a rallying point, and under his able command it played a significant role as the Allies retrieved their fortunes in this vital theatre.

Layton was promoted to admiral in 1942, and in 1945 returned to the UK to be Commander-in-Chief, Portsmouth. During his tenure he commented, at a naval gathering in 1945, that the Royal Navy did not favour conscription as a means of filling its ranks. When he spoke he was expressing a view held by every general and air marshal too. Those remarks, made over sixty years ago, are as valid today as when Geoffrey Layton made them, because everyone knows that conscription, for a short period of two years, turns the armed forces into a vast training machine, with a commensurate and deleterious effect on its fighting capacity. Nevertheless, a Major Donald Bruce,[5] the Member of Parliament for Portsmouth North, one of Layton's local MPs and very recently elected as a Labour member, made an issue of the Admiral's remarks and raised the matter in the House of Commons. It was solemnly agreed that Layton should not have spoken so openly (albeit correctly), but that his conduct was not sufficiently grave as to require disciplinary action against him. Layton was still appointed KCMG that year.

In 1947, and now aged 62, Adm Sir Geoffrey Layton retired with the final distinction of GBE. He went to live at Rowland's Castle, a village in Hampshire within easy striking distance of Portsmouth and all his old haunts. He lived contentedly there until his death in 1964, aged 80.

His very detailed and voluminous obituary, published in *The Times*, made no mention of the events central to this book and of the part he had played in them – but that is easily explained, because the 'Battle of the Isle of May' was still shrouded in secrecy, and a further thirty years were going to have to elapse before those events became public knowledge.

Captain James Rose Price Hawksley CB CVO
Captain of HMS Inflexible

James Hawksley is one of the great unknowns of this story. He was not a man favoured with either exceptional talent or obvious high social standing and influence. All the indications are that he was no more than an average officer (see page 51). He patently misled the Court of Inquiry, and despite this was never challenged – at least there is nothing either on the file or on his personal documents to say so.

It is possible that behind closed doors and off the record his performance was reassessed, although there is nothing on his personal file to this effect. It is no more than speculation, but his early retirement *might* have been the result of such a reassessment.

James Hawksley had married Gertrude Emily Rose Price in 1899, when he was 28, and it must be presumed that he added part of her name to his on the occasion of their marriage. James Hawksley had been promoted captain in 1912, and at the age of 41 he made his name at the Battle of Jutland, when he commanded a destroyer flotilla. He performed to such effect that he was Mentioned in Dispatches and appointed CB. He commanded *Inflexible* for two years until March 1919.

With the coming of peace, the opportunity for sea-going appointments was reduced, and in 1920 Hawksley was sent to Portland to be Captain in charge. This was his last job, and having served here for two years he retired in 1922, aged 51. He was promoted rear admiral on retirement, and in 1928 was advanced to vice-admiral. His documents carry the stark entry 'DD 7.4.55'. This is Royal Navy speak for 'Discharged dead 7 April 1955'. He did indeed die at Camberley, Surrey, on that date, aged 84.

Lieutenant Richard Douglas Sandford
Officer of the Watch, K-6

Sandford was probably a little aggrieved at the blame placed upon him for the collision with *K-4*, but the naval establishment obviously had great faith in him, and he did not have time to mope because he was selected to command HM Submarine *C-3* in the attack on Zeebrugge on 23 April 1918.

The ever-present threat posed by German submarines had to be curtailed, and to this end Rear Adm Roger Keyes devised a plan to immobilize the main U-boat base at Bruges by blocking its access to the sea. Keyes planned to suppress local defences so that three block ships could sail past and scuttle themselves in the exit of the Bruges–Zeebrugge canal, thus sealing the U boats in their base and denying them free range in the North Sea This was the now famous attack on Zeebrugge.

The success of the operation rested on the destruction of a single, metal viaduct. This bridge-like construction connected the mole, which was the location of the main harbour defences, to the shore. The destruction of this viaduct would prevent any reinforcements getting to the mole. If the plan succeeded it would give valuable support to the attack by the British assault troops who were to be landed directly onto the mole, and allow the block ships unhindered passage.

It was decided that an old submarine, its bow filled with five tons of Amatol, could be driven in among the support girders of the viaduct and then detonated. A simple plan, and two old submarines, *C-1* and *C-3*, were selected and prepared for the task, but mishaps affected *C-1*, and she did not complete the voyage to the target. It was *C-3* alone, under the command of Lt Sandford, which was left to complete the mission.

Lieutenant R.D. Sandford VC.
(www.dropbears.com)

Under the cover of smoke and darkness Sandford made his stealthy approach to the viaduct, but the wind suddenly changed, blew away his smoke cover and left him, still with a mile and a half to run, in full view and close under the German guns. Nevertheless, *C-3*, with her 'getaway skiff' securely mounted alongside the conning tower in a bizarre harness, made an unhindered approach with a great battle being fought about half a mile away on the mole. This intense action was illuminated by star shells and Very lights fired by both sides, and they did serve to cast some intermittent light over the whole area. Sandford set a course straight for the centre of the mole, and then he ordered his skeleton crew onto the casing. It later transpired that the Germans thought *C-3* was trying to enter the harbour, and they held their fire as the capture of the submarine and crew seemed likely.

Sandford corrected his course, and *C-3*'s bow drove violently into the viaduct and her impetus sliced through the supporting girders. HM Submarine *C-3* came to rest with her explosive-laden bows exactly in the right position. Sandford ordered his crew to lower the skiff provided for their escape, and which by happy chance had not been holed. The crew scrambled into the skiff, and then, last to leave, Sandford set the twelve-minute fuse.

By this time the Germans had realized what was intended, and opened fire on the skiff. Two members of the crew were hit and Sandford, at the tiller, was hit twice. Stemming the current, they had gone only a short distance when *C-3*

Lieutenant Sandford on the casing of HM Submarine C-3 before the raid. (www.dropbears.com)

exploded. Debris fell all around the small boat, but fortunately no one was injured. A significant breach was cut in the viaduct and the German troops, now isolated at the seaward end of the mole, were never reinforced.

Meanwhile the small crew of HM Submarine C-3 was eventually picked up by Lt Cdr F.H. Sandford (the elder brother of Richard) in a rescue boat. All of them survived.

Each of the four ratings was decorated with the CGM, Lt Howell-Price received the DSO and Lt Sandford was awarded the Victoria Cross. Richard Sandford recovered from his wounds, but sadly he did not live long to enjoy his

The effect of Sandford's attack on the Zeebrugge viaduct, which prevented the movement of German reinforcements towards the heavily defended end of the mole (left).

fame. He died of typhoid fever on 23 November 1918, less than two weeks after the guns fell silent.

Commander Ernest William Leir DSO
Captain of HMS **Ithuriel** *and Commander of 13th Submarine Flotilla*

Ernest Leir picked up where he had left off after those celebratory drinks in *Ithuriel*'s wardroom. He continued in command of the 13th SF until March 1919, when he took command of the 12th SF. He was decorated with the Légion d'honneur that same year and was promoted to captain in June.

He did a two-year tour as Assistant Captain of Chatham Dockyard and King's Harbour Master. He then commanded HMS *Triad* in the Persian Gulf from February 1924 until April 1926. His career blossomed, and an appointment as Capt (D)[6] occupied him until 1928. His seagoing came to an end and he filled several administrative jobs until he was appointed ADC to the King and promoted to rear admiral on retirement in October 1931.

Leir volunteered to rejoin the service in 1939, and served most effectively for three hard years spent at sea and in constant action. He was Mentioned in Dispatches in 1942 for 'Outstanding devotion to duty during three years' arduous service as a Commodore of ocean convoys'. This had been stressful and demanding work, and then, aged 60, he retired for the second time.

No more might have been heard of Ernst Leir had he not attracted public notice, as the newspaper cutting opposite shows.

Ernest Leir had lived in Ditcheat since he was eight, and in 1952 he was 69. The vicar was new to the parish – a parish in which the Leir family had played a significant part for over several hundred years – and he and his parishioner could not agree on some religious issues or on the manner in which parish affairs were conducted. The parson had failed to respond to letters from the Admiral, which had incensed him. The final straw was when, on 23 March, Leir believed that the second lesson read in church was meant to apply to him. The assault followed. After the assault he had made an approach in an effort to apologise, but the apology was not accepted.

The Leir family coat of arms (*Provided by Rick Leir*)

Category: News
Full Text: Copyright 1952, The Times

ALLEGED ASSAULT ON RECTOR

REAR-ADMIRAL SENT FOR TRIAL

At Shepton Mallet, Somerset, yesterday REAR-ADMIRAL ERNEST WILLIAM LEIR (retd.), 70, of South Hill, Ditcheat, was charged with unlawfully striking a clergyman, the Rev. Harold George Cole, rector of Ditcheat—who, to his knowledge, was returning from celebrating divine service in the parish church of Ditcheat—contrary to section 36 of the Offences Against the Persons Act, 1861.

Mr. Douglas Wild, for the prosecution, said that the alleged offence occurred on Sunday morning, March 23. The rector officiated at a service and was assisted by the Rev. L. C. Margerison. Rear-Admiral Leir left his place in the congregation in the course of the service.

After the service the two clergymen were crossing the road when the Rear-Admiral asked the rector when he was going to get a reply to some letters, and was told " in due course." The clergymen then went to their car. The Rear-Admiral said the rector was " not going to get away with it," and he lay down by the back wheels of the car, which was parked with its nose against the wall. At first the rector could not start his car, as he had forgotten to turn on the ignition. When he did so the car at the third attempt sprang into life, and apparently so did the Admiral, because he was lying just under the exhaust.

The Rear-Admiral then got up, went to the front of the car, and rained blows on the rector, who was left with blood flowing from his nose and lacerations of the upper lip. The rector offered no resistance, but simply turned his head to one side.

Rear-Admiral Leir, who reserved his defence, was committed for trial at Bridgwater Quarter Sessions on April 25.

A cutting from *The Times* of 10 April 1952. (*The Times*)

The solicitor acting for Ernest Leir told the court that, 'The facts of this case are before the Admiralty and it may be that the Admiralty will take action with regard to his pension.' The final entry on this old sailor's service record is to chronicle his conviction. There is no record of any review of his pension, gallantly earned, nor should there have been. The admiral duly appeared before the bench, pleaded 'Guilty', and was fined £20 and ordered to pay the costs of the Prosecution.

Ernest Leir, the man whose decision to turn his flotilla westward had been crucial in this story of 'The Battle of the Isle of May', died where he had grown up and spent his latter years, in Ditcheat, Somerset, on 2 August 1971, aged 88.

Rear Admiral Leir, aged about 80. *(Leir family)*

Notes

1. The practice of promoting officers on retirement and then promoting them further on a time basis would have done wonders for the ego of the recipients of an unearned promotion. The system was not applied evenly to all, and Slayter, whose rank when serving was captain, died a full-blown admiral. Leir, on the other hand, also a captain, went no further than rear admiral.
2. None of the officers promoted on the retired list and named in this book were recalled, in World War II, to serve in their higher rank.
3. But then so, too, to a lesser degree, did Nelson.
4. This is extraordinary. Why a CB (civil) should have been awarded to a naval officer is inexplicable. He probably had just the one medal but two ribbons!
5. When Bruce lost his seat in 1950 he failed to find another seat, but eventually, in 1974, Harold Wilson made him a life peer and he became Lord Bruce of Donington. He was described in an obituary as 'long winded'. He died in 2005, aged 93.
6. A Captain (D) is the commander of a flotilla or squadron of destroyers.

The K Boats

The object of this book is not to chronicle the ill-fated K-class submarines. That has been done, in detail, elsewhere However, their performance and characteristics are such that the 'Battle of The Isle of May' would not have taken place without their presence. That being the case, it is appropriate to fit these boats into their historical context, and in so doing, the rapid development of a Royal Navy submarine force from 1900 should be considered.

By 1900, although submarines of various degrees of effectiveness had been on the foreign scene for over fifty years, it was only reluctantly that the Royal Navy accepted that this new war engine might just have a part to play. The Admiralty viewed submarines with disfavour, and, as the century turned, the greatest navy on earth did not have a single submarine. The naval establishment's attention was focused on big ships with big guns.

However, in 1901 the Admiralty took note of the work of an American designer called Holland, and commissioned five 'Holland' boats for experimental purposes. The first submarine in the Royal Navy, of 120 tons, was *H-1*. She was built by Vickers Ltd and launched in November 1901, and is today to be seen at the Royal Navy Submarine Museum in Gosport. The visitor can but stand and wonder that men trusted their lives to craft such as this.

The H class was followed by A, B, C, and D classes, and there was a progression in size to 530 tons. By 1910 a total of sixty boats had been built. There had, however, been attrition, and eight boats had been lost, five of them to collision with surface ships.

The E class was introduced in 1912, and this was really no more that an adapted and enlarged D-class boat. It was a sizeable vessel of almost 800 tons. Nine E-class vessels were built, and they were based in Harwich.

When war was declared in 1914, Britain was equipped with sixty-four submarines, but only seventeen were 'blue water' boats, and the remaining forty-seven were judged to be suitable only for defensive purposes around the coast of Britain. The Intelligence Service reported that the Germans were vastly better prepared with bigger, faster submarines, and many more of them. The intelligence was inaccurate but it was enough to galvanize the Admiralty in general and Adm Sir Jackie Fisher in particular. The J class was produced, but did not meet its specifications, and it led to the concept of the steam-driven submarine.

It is against this background that the K-class boat evolved. Those who sailed in these boats described them as a 'death-trap in heavy seas, water came over the top of the two funnels and into air intake valves flooding the boiler room causing boiler flashbacks and putting out the fires'. It was apparently quite normal for oilskins to be worn inside the boat when at sea. This state of affairs should surely have sent a signal to someone that perhaps these boats were not up to the job.

'Dive, Dive, and Dive' – an order that took seconds to accomplish in other classes of submarine – took over five minutes in a K boat. Capt Blackburn reported to John Barry (*Naval battles that never were*, by Rev. John Barry, 1990) that after giving the order to dive, 'There was time enough for the Captain to take a gentle stroll around the upper works to ensure that everything was in order before himself descending into the control room and closing the hatch behind him.'

Someone famously summed up the K boats as having 'the speed of a destroyer, the turning circle of a battlecruiser and the control facilities of a picket boat'. Nevertheless the Royal Navy organized these fast but vulnerable submarines with poor control systems into flotillas, and then incorporated them as an integral part of a fast-moving, highly manoeuvrable surface fleet. Now, after almost a hundred years and armed with 20/20 hindsight, it makes no sense.

It is conceded that these were early days in submarine warfare, but, nevertheless, the seamen who made the decisions to employ them in this manner made an extraordinary mistake. A mistake that was not publicly admitted, for as late as 1921 a report was published which said with breathtaking complacency, 'The K boats had always fulfilled the functions for which they were designed.' This was not a view shared by the unfortunates who had to crew these boats.

The class did have its adherents. Earlier, in 1919, *The Naval Review* published an article written in defence of the K boats. If the unnamed author of this essay is to be believed, the philosophy that underpinned the tactical employment of these boats was based upon the overrated value of speed, rampant supposition, pious hopes and overwhelming optimism. In the interests of balance it is quoted here in full.

The appreciations of the tactics at Jutland showed how imperative it is to have 'Fleet submarines'. The first and principal essential required for this work is sufficient speed to be able to keep the speed of the Fleet in most weathers and, to get this, quick-diving qualities had to be sacrificed in the same way that armour and guns were sacrificed in Battlecruisers.[1]

Remembering that speed is all important it is seen that the K boat design is highly successful, a speed of 24 knots being obtained which is sufficient to allow for 20 knots being kept up in moderate weather. Critics who maintain that in bad weather the speed must be reduced to a crawl have scarcely studied the question from a large enough standpoint.

In a case of urgency a K boat can keep up a speed of 19–20 knots in weather that would force destroyers to reduce to 15 knots or break up. Admittedly, damage to the bridge and superstructure must be expected and the stokers in the boiler-room would suffer severe discomfort from water pouring down the air intakes and funnels, sometimes extinguishing the fires (which can very quickly be relighted). The main point is that the ½-inch hull will not suffer from any amount of overdriving in bad weather like the thin plating of a destroyer so unless the Commander-in-Chief was willing to leave his destroyers, he would never outpace his K boats.

Having this speed makes it possible for K boats to get into an attacking position before the battleship duel begins – no other submarine could do this. Those[2] that left harbour at the same time as the Fleet would not arrive until the action was over, and those already on patrol near enough to see the enemy would not have sufficient speed to place themselves in an attacking position unless by chance they were already there.

Given the necessary speed, the other essentials are as large a number of torpedo tubes as possible (which was fulfilled by building four bow and four beam) and a good tactician as Captain (S) for the flotilla leader in a light cruiser …

In the battle formation of the Grand Fleet, during the war the K boats were stationed 10 miles ahead of the main battle squadrons with various light forces spread out ahead of them to a distance of about 25 miles.

On the screening forces sighting the enemy and reporting by W/T the Captain (S) had to manoeuvre to place his flotilla ahead of the probable course of the enemy battle fleet and if possible, slightly on the side furthest from our own heavy ships.

When in position the boats were detached in pairs to act independently. Generally, at least three pairs could be counted on as being present. The distance between them varying according to circumstances to ensure that two pairs got in their attack even if the enemy made a considerable alteration in course.

The boats of a pair then separated to about one mile by previous arrangement, to avoid the chances of underwater collision, and prepared for diving. When the leading enemy ships were about four miles off the boats would dive, taking at most five minutes, as they would be already trimmed down. It must be remembered that the conning tower, end-on, is very difficult to see in calm weather at two miles, and in action the firing of our light forces would probably distract the attention of enemy lookouts sufficiently to ensure the K boats being unobserved.[3]

After diving the range of action is very much restricted and unless the Captain (S) had slipped the boats into the correct positions the enemy would pass out of range of the boats which can only proceed at seven knots when submerged. Should the boats be in the correct position the action radius of seven knots for about one hour would be more than sufficient, as the high speed would not much be required, and long before an hour had elapsed the action would have passed over the horizon.

Unless the enemy turned 16 points shortly after the K boats dived, they must pass close to them,[4] or else turn away toward our own battle fleet, either procedure suiting the Commander-in-Chief whose tactics would be formed accordingly.

Taking the first case of proceeding on the same course or turning slightly away from our battle fleet; the K boats would find themselves in an ideal attacking position from which experienced captains could not fail to obtain at least 60% of hits and probably would obtain 90%.

Imagine 29 torpedoes hitting before the gun duel had even begun!

If the enemy turned towards our battle fleet or turned 16 points when 4,000 yards away, the submarines could still fire 'browning' salvoes of torpedoes set for 19 knots which by the laws of chance, at least 25% would hit, and several ships would probably be damaged enough to be unable to keep in the line.

Even if the submarines were sighted during the attack only capital ships could ram them if at periscope depth and in the unlikely event of destroyers carrying depth charges during a fleet action, it seems improbable that many boats would be sunk before they had time to fire their torpedoes.

The time taken to reload the tubes makes it unlikely that many 'second shots' could be fired before the enemy had passed out of range; the boats would then, after attacking stragglers, concentrate on a prearranged line off the enemy coast to intercept returning ships.

Critics also deride the usefulness of K boats on patrol, forgetting that to be present in a fleet action is the primary cause of their existence – patrols were a secondary consideration introduced chiefly for exercising the boats, which were found to suffer from numerous minor breakdowns after too long a period in harbour. From this point of view patrols were most beneficial, the average number of effective boats being nearly doubled after a few weeks of patrols. The duty of a K boat on patrol is rather different to any other submarine on look-out duty.

Should an enemy vessel be sighted the K boat reports at once, and probably has finished her signal and 'trimmed down' before she is seen herself and can then get to periscope depth in four minutes. Her hull being under water in less than two minutes the chances of a shell damaging her inner hull when in this position is extremely remote especially at short range when shells would burst or ricochet on the water or her outer hull. The superstructure might be shot to pieces without doing more than flood the conning tower and lower funnels, which could easily be adjusted for in the trim.

The objections to the discomforts of living in on the boat, and of being 'one of a crowd' instead of having a little action alone and consequently reaping all the credit, are both obvious and true; but the writer hopes that this essay will save K boats from a little of the unmerited ridicule heaped on them by so many submarine officers who, in many cases, have never seen one, and have no conception of their duties and tactics in action.

To sum up in brief the use of K boats, it may be said that: As surface ships, they can get to the scene of action and choose their attacking position, after which they have, except for a small difference of speed, the same chance of making a successful attack as any other submarine in the same position.

The naivety of the author of the above essay, which was published in a professional journal, is breathtaking. If the theories that he expounds were held by the upper echelons of the Royal Navy it is probably as well that they were never put into practice.

Any judgment made upon the K boats must be based upon their effectiveness as a weapon of war. By this criterion the K class failed because it did not sink a single German ship nor did it kill a single German sailor.

The boats were produced at enormous cost (over £6 million) and took up a significant slice of the Navy estimates, but their greatest legacy is the toll they took of British sailors. It is estimated that 350 officers and men lost their lives while serving in these boats, none as a result of enemy action – all due to some form of mechanical failure that was a direct result of an inherently ill-judged design.

One observer, D. Everitt, commented that, 'I never met anyone who had the least affection for the K class, and they were looked on with fear and loathing.'

The very last word on the subject is from Ernest Leir, who summed it all up when he said, late in his life, 'It was just as well that the K boats never engaged the enemy.'

K-26, the last of the K boats. The photograph illustrates how the bow was rebuilt to contend, at least in part, with heavy seas that had confounded earlier boats by flooding the control room and dowsing the boilers. Contrast this photograph with that of *K-3* on page 37. *(Submariners' Association)*

The fate of the K boats

K-1 Sunk by HMS *Blonde* after collision with *K-4*	1917
K-2 Collided with *K-12*, collided with *H-29*	1924
Sold for breaking	1926
K-3 Uncontrolled dive during diving trials	
Sold for breaking	1921
K-4 Sunk in collision with *K-6*. Fifty-five killed	1918
K-5 Uncontrolled dive	
Sunk in unknown circumstances. Fifty-seven killed	1921
K-6 Collided with and sank *K-4*	1918
Sold for breaking	1926
K-7 Sold for breaking	1921
K-8 Damaged by fire, sold for breaking	1923
K-9 Failed to dive, sold for breaking	1926
K-10 Sold for breaking	1921
K-11 Sold for breaking	1921
K-12 Collided with *K-2*	1924
Sold for breaking	1926
K-13 Foundered. Thirty-five killed	1917
Raised and renumbered *K-22*	1917
Collided with *K-14*	1918
Dived with funnels up and almost lost	
Broken up	1927
K-14 Collided with *K-22*, two men killed	1918
Boiler explosion caused extensive damage	
Sold for breaking	1926

The submarine originally ordered as *K-18* but reconfigured and named *M-1*. The extraordinary feature of this boat is its 12-inch gun. *(Illustrated London News Picture Library)*

The original *K-19*, which, although originally cancelled, was eventually built and launched as *M-2*. Seen here launching a seaplane. *(Wikipedia)*

K-15 Uncontrolled first dive, stern first
Sunk in Portsmouth harbour, all saved
Sold for breaking   1924
K-16 Uncontrolled dive on trials, sold for breaking   1924
K-17 Sunk in collision with HMS *Fearless*. Forty-seven killed   1918
K-18 Cancelled 1917 but built and redesignated *M-1*   1918
Sunk with about sixty killed after collision with a Swedish ship[5]   1925
K-19 Cancelled   1917
But built and redesignated *M-2*   1918
Sunk on exercise, the reason unknown. Sixty killed   1932
K-20 Cancelled   1917
K-21 Cancelled   1917
Then ordered and to be redesignated *M-4*   1917
Cancelled again   1917
K-26 Acceptance trials accident. Two killed   1923
Sold for breaking   1931

Notes
1. …and what happened to the battlecruisers is very well recorded.
2. Other classes of submarines.
3. The writer seems to have forgotten the smoke signature of these boats, which did nothing to aid concealment.
4. No account seems to have been taken of the enemy's screening destroyers.
5. The wreck of *M-1* was not found until 1990, off Start Point.

Appendix Two

The Roll of Honour

Consequent on the sinking of HM Submarines *K-4* and *K-17* and the damage inflicted on *K-14* on 31 January 1918, 104 officers and ratings died. Their names and personal details are listed here in order to put a human face on a tragic event.

They are also remembered on various war memorials, as the list below shows.[1]

HM Submarine K-4
4 Officers and 51 Ratings

CHATHAM NAVAL MEMORIAL

ADAMS, Petty Officer Stoker, PERCY WALTER. *DSM*. Age 34. Son of William and Harriett Adams of Woodbridge. Husband of Constance E. Adams of 25, Union St, St Michael's, Ipswich.

BIRMINGHAM (HANDSWORTH) CEMETERY

BEER, Chief Stoker, FRANK JOHN, Age 35. Husband of Maud Beer, of 82, Jefferson Rd, Sheerness, Kent.

BOUNDS, Stoker 1st Class, HORACE. *DSM*. Age 25. Son of Walter and Mary Louisa Bounds, of 'Donalda', Love St, Eddington, Herne Bay.

BROWN, Stoker 1st Class, CHARLES EDWARD.

BURT, Able Seaman, ERNEST SAMUEL. Age 23. Son of John and Sophia Burt, of 8, Ranelagh Rd, Wood Green, London.

CORFIELD, Petty Officer, ALFRED ABE BENJAMIN.

DUGGAN, Able Seaman, ALAN MONTGOMERIE.

GODDARD, Able Seaman, CHARLES WILLIAM HENRY. Age 26. Son of Alexander Charles and Lucy Goddard, of London. Husband of Janet Pickthall (formerly Goddard), of 11, Long Row, Trinkelt Cottage, Swarthmoor, Ulverston, Lancs.

GOODSALL, Leading Stoker, JOHN HENRY. *Mentioned in Dispatches*. Age 24. Son of George and Kate Goodsall of 3, Peels Place, Ashford Rd, Tenterden, Kent.

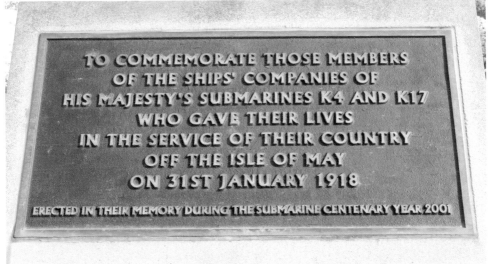

The memorial at Anstruther harbour.[1] *(Author)*

GRANT, Stoker 1st Class, PATRICK JOSEPH. *Mentioned in Dispatches*. Age 25. Son of Patrick and Rose Grant, of Liverpool.

HAYES, Stoker 1st Class, JOSEPH CHARLES. Age 24. Son of Joseph Hayes, of Belfast. Husband of Minnie Hayes, of 5, Shaftesbury St, Belfast.

HOGG, Leading Seaman, ALBERT EDWARD. Age 25. Native of Tottenham, London.

IRON, Leading Stoker, JAMES THOMAS. *DSM*. Age 35. Son of George and Eliza Iron, of Haverhill. Husband of Matilda Iron, of 47, High St, Haverhill, Suffolk.

MARTIN, Stoker 1st Class, HERBERT ERNEST. Age 24. Son of George and Bessie Martin, of The Square, Purton, Swindon, Wilts. Native of Lambeth, London.

PEARSON, Leading Seaman, ALFRED EDWARD. *DSM*.

PUDDEFOOT, Able Seaman, ERNEST JAMES. Age 23. Son of Mr. and Mrs Puddefoot, of 50, Holywell Rd, Watford, Herts. Husband of Rose Puddefoot, of 2, St Mary's Villas, Church Rd, Northwood, Middx.

RIVETT, Able Seaman, LEONARD WILLIAM.

SPICE, Able Seaman, ALBERT. Age 27. *Awarded Africa General Service Medal (Somaliland Clasp) and Naval General Service Medal (Persian Gulf)*. Son of Harry and E. Spice, of 78, Hartfield Crescent, Wimbledon, London.

SPICE, Able Seaman, JOHN. Age 36. Son of Mr H. and Mrs F. Spice, 48, Bygrove St, Merton, Surrey.

TREDGETT, Stoker 1st Class, JAMES HENRY.

VAREY, Artificer 4th Class, ALAN M. Age 23. Son of Charles and Annie Varey, of 44, Alfred St, Bury, Lancs.

WINDIBANK, Able Seaman, ALBERT CHARLES. Age 22. Son of the late John Windibank, of Headley Park, Borden, Hants. Husband of Mary Elizabeth Jenner (formerly Windibank), of 64, Holydale Rd, Peckham. London.

WOOD, Leading Stoker, THOMAS STEWART.

YOUNG, Able Seaman, THOMAS SIDNEY. Age 21. Son of Mr S.H.Young, of 19, Marmion Terrace, Monkseaton, Northumberland.

PLYMOUTH NAVAL MEMORIAL

BALDWIN, Petty Officer Telegraphist, GEORGE HAROLD. Age 23. Son of George and Mary Baldwin, of Kennels, Kineton, Warwick. Native of Longthorpe, Northants.

CARTER, Leading Signalman, CHARLES. *DSM*. Son of Edith Carter, of 'The Cabin', Kings Rd, Blandford, Dorset, and the late Thomas Carter.

COCKERILL, Stoker 1st Class, PERCIVAL. Age 23. Son of John H. and Minnie Cockerill, of 37, Laburnum Avenue, Garden Village, Hull.

DANGERFLELD, Able Seaman, WILLIAM GEORGE. Age 20. Son of Edward and Mary Dangerfield, of 1, Prison Quarters, Bodmin, Cornwall. Native of Portsmouth.

GODDARD, Engine Room Artificer 4th Class, HENRY THORPE. Age 25. Son of Henry and F. S. Goddard, of Duncannon Cottage, Stoke Gabriel, Totnes, Devon. A native of Great Grimsby.

HAYMAN, Leading Stoker, WILLIAM HENRY. Age 34. Husband of Mary Rachel Hayman, of 3, Vigo Bridge, Tavistock.

WALKER, Leading Telegraphist, FREDERICK. Age 26. Son of Robert and Agnes Walker, of Dale Abbey, Ilkeston, Derbyshire.

PORTSMOUTH NAVAL MEMORIAL

ADAMS, Chief Engine Room Artificer 2nd Class, LEONARD. *DSM*. Husband of Norah Adams, of 65, Copnor Rd, Copnor, Portsmouth.

APPS, Engine Room Artificer 1st Class, JOHN FREDERICK. *DSM*. Age 27. Son of John Apps, of 77, Leicester Rd, East Finchley, London.

ARMSTRONG, Able Seaman, JAMES. Age 23. Son of George and Sarah Armstrong, of Stow, Lincoln.

BLAKE, Able Seaman, STANLEY HAROLD. Age 33. Son of John and Elizabeth Blake, of Northampton. Husband of Louisa Blake, of 198, Oxford Gardens, Stafford.

BURGESS, Stoker 1st Class, ALBERT CHARLES. Age 25. Son of the late Mr and Mrs Henry Burgess, of Ashe, Basingstoke, Hants. Husband of Edith R. Burgess, of Southdown, Medstead, Alton, Hants.

CASE, Chief Petty Officer, CHARLES. *DSM*.

CHURCH, Leading Stoker, WILLIAM. *DSM*.

CRAWFORTH, Stoker 1st Class, HARRY WAKELIN. Age 21. Son of William and Ada Emma Crawforth, of 2, Mentone Avenue, Arundel St, Holderness Rd, Hull, Yorks.

FENNER, Lt Cdr, ATHELSTAN ALFRED LENNOX, Age 31. First Lieutenant of HM Submarine *K-4* Son of Dr Robert Fenner and Edith Fenner (née Carter), of 38, Portland Place, London. Born at Cromer, Norfolk.

HAMMOND, Gunner, JOHN WILLIAM, H. Age 32. Son of John F.B. Hammond. Husband of Sarah Elizabeth Hammond, of 8, Markland Rd, Dover.

HANKS, Stoker 1st Class, FREDERICK FRANCIS. Age 24. Son of William Arthur Frederick Hanks, of 19, Mawbey Rd, Old Kent Rd, London.

HILL, Artificer Electrical 2nd Class, RALPH REUBEN. Age 41. Son of Samuel Hill, Farmer, of Dursley, Glos. Husband of Margaret A. Hill, of 72, Bramshott Rd, Goldsmith Avenue, Portsmouth.

JACKSON, Able Seaman, THOMAS WILLIAM. *DSM*. Age 32. Son of Thomas and Alice Jackson, of Marlow. Husband of Edith Ellen Jackson, of 29, South Place, Marlow, Bucks.

LEEDER, Able Seaman, EDWARD BARBER.

MOCKFORD, Able Seaman, FRED.

ROWLEY, Petty Officer, WILLIAM. *DSM*.

SHEATH, Petty Officer Stoker, HARRY. *DSM.* Age 38. Son of Charlotte Sheath, of 56, Highfield St, Fratton. Husband of Annie Gertrude Sheath, of 9, Highfield St, Fratton, Portsmouth.

STOCKS, Cdr, DAVID DE BEAUVOIR. *DSO. Chevalier, Légion d'honneur* (France). Age 34. The Captain of HM Submarine *K-4*. Son of John Wallace Stocks (late Capt B.H. Light Horse), and Elizabeth Brock, his wife of Sutton, Surrey. Husband of Cheridah A. Stocks, of Westcombe, Evercreech, Somerset.

WATKINS, Signalman, MALCOLM POYNTER.

WATTERSON, Lt, THOMAS ARTHUR, *DSC*, RNR Age 27. Son of John and Clara Watterson, of Liverpool. Husband of Marian Watterson, of 42, Dinmore Rd, Wallasey, Cheshire.

WELLESLEY, Lt, CLAUD MICHAEL ASHMORE. Age 27. Son of Maj. E.H.C. and Mrs C.I. Wellesley, of Bromley, Kilpedder, Co. Wicklow.

WYATT, Petty Officer Stoker, WILLIAM THOMAS. *DSM.*

YOUDALE, Officer's Steward, HAROLD WILLIAM. Age 24. Son of William and Anne Youdale, of 29, Beaconsfield Rd, Brighton, Sussex.

WOODS, Engine Room Artificer 2nd Class, GEORGE OLIVER CHARLES. Age 31. Son of George and Carrie Woods, of Portsmouth. Husband of Annie Woods, of 42, Bramshott Rd, Southsea, Portsmouth.

The *K-4* memorial in St Margaret Patten Church, Eastcheap, London. *(G.S.T. Nash)*

The inscription reads 'To the proud and undying remembrance of my husband Commdr. De Beauvoir Stocks RN *DSO Legion d'honneur* who was drowned January 31st 1918 serving his King and Country and in memory of all of those who died with him.'[2]

HM Submarine K-17
5 Officers and 42 men
(1 officer and 8 men were saved)

BIRMINGHAM (HANDSWORTH) CEMETERY

HAMMOND, Able Seaman, FRANCIS. Age 23. Son of Joseph and Ellen Hammond of 49, Spring Rd, Edgbaston, Birmingham. Grave Ref. 3D. 5469.

ANTRAM, Lt, HERBERT WILKINS. Age 25. Son of the Rev. C.E.P. and Mrs Antram. Husband of Marjorie Lester Antram of 'The Vicarage,' Blean, Canterbury.

BINNINGTON, Stoker 1st Class, CHARLES EDWARD. Age 24. Son of Henrietta Binnington of 10, Sea View Terrace, North Gate, Hunmanby, Yorks.

BROWN, Engine Room Artif. 4th Class, JACK GLANFIELD. Age 29. Son of John Brown and Henrietta Brown of 6 Gibson St, Ipswich.

CARESS, Stoker 1st Class, HENRY ALFRED.

CARTER, Stoker 1st Class, WILLIAM JAMES FREDERICK.

COOK, Leading Stoker, WILLIAM JAMES. Age 28. Son of George Ambrose and Rose Cook, of Plumstead, London. Husband of Lily Cook, of 41, Albion Rd, Woolwich, London.

COOPER, Leading Signalman, WILLIAM WILCOX. Age 27. Son of the late George Cooper, Station Officer, of St Andrews Coast Guard Station.

DE BANK, Stoker 1st Class, ARTHUR GEORGE DAVID. Age 22. Son of Rhoda Rebecca de Bank, of 1, Model Cottages, Horn Lane, Woodford Green, Essex, and the late James William de Bank.

DRAKE, Able Seaman, ARTHUR RAYMENT. Age 28. Son of Mr H. Drake, of 16, St Philip's Rd, Newmarket, Suffolk.

HEARN, Lt Cdr, HENRY JOHN, *Mentioned in Dispatches*, The Captain H.M. Submarine *K.-17*, Age 32. Son of Henry John and Laura Jane Hearn, of 'Bycroft', Church Stretton, Shropshire. Native of Shrewsbury.

HERRING, Engine Room Artificer 4th Class, HAROLD LOUIS. Age 32. Son of Horace and Jane Herring, of London. Husband of Victoria Herring, of 45A, Sinclair Rd, West Kensington, London.

KNIGHT, Leading Telegraphist, GEORGE ALEXANDER..Age 23. Son of Charles and Mary Knight, of 34, Helise Rd, Brixton, London.

LIGHTBODY, Able Seaman, HENRY GEORGE. Age 22. Husband of Jessie Hannah Louise Lightbody of 28, Redman Buildings, Bourne Estate, Holborn, London.

McDONALD, Stoker 1st Class, JOHN RIDDELL. Age 24. Son of Hugh and Sarah McDonald, of Central Fire Station, 82, Chichester St, Belfast.

MEADMORE, Leading Seaman, EDWARD JAMES. *DSM*.

MORRIS, Petty Officer Stoker, ERNEST. Age 29. Son of W.E. and H. Morris, of West End Cottage, Marden, Kent.

NETTLETON, Able Seaman, HAROLD. Age 22. Son of Ada Gilbertson (formerly Nettleton), of 20, Woodbine St, Ossett, Yorks, and the late John William Nettleton.

SAMUEL, Able Seaman, FREDERICK. Age 23. Son of Henry and Louisa Samuel, of 89, Clementina Rd, Leyton, London.

SANGSTER, Stoker 1st Class, LEO FREDERICK MURRAY. *Mentioned in Dispatches*. Age 22. Son of Ellen Annie Sangster, of 1A, Post Office Cottages, Thames Rd, Chiswick, London, and the late Harry Sangster.

SINFIELD, Leading Seaman, ALBERT EDWARD. Age 25. (Served as SIMPSON). Son of Mr and Mrs T.J. Sinfield, of East Greenwich. Husband of Ellen Elizabeth Sinfield, of 19, Caletock St, East Greenwich, London.

TYRRELL, Lt, HUGO WILLIAM LOUIS. Age 26. Son of Sir William and Lady Tyrrell, of 36, Egerton Crescent, Chelsea, London..

WARDE, Lt, CECIL.

PLYMOUTH NAVAL MEMORIAL

ADAMS, Engine Room Artificer 3rd Class, ALBERT VICTOR. Age 31. Son of William and Susan Mary Adams, of 'Tatham,' Garfield Rd, Paignton. A native of New Kingsbridge, Devon.

AGNEW, Able Seaman, WILLIAM.

BERRIMAN, Able Seaman, THOMAS HENRY. Age 33. Holder of *The Long Service and Good Conduct Medal*. Brother of Mrs R.M. White, of 21, Granby St, Devonport.

CUNNINGHAM, Midshipman, E.S.R., Royal Australian Navy.

GALE, Leading Stoker, WILLIAM JOHN.

GIBBS, Able Seaman, JOHN. Age 24. Son of John and Eliza Gibbs, of 5, Otley Terrace, Lea Bridge Rd, Clapton, London.

GIBSON, Chief Engine Room Artificer 2nd Class, ISAAC. Age 39. Son of Samuel and Charlotte Gibson, of Belfast. Husband of Ellen Duncan Gibson, of 38, Sidney St, Saltcoats, Ayrshire.

HOSKING, Leading Seaman, CECIL JAMES.

KNOWLES, Stoker 1st Class, JAMES EDWARD. Age 24. Son of John Henry and Margaret Ann Knowles, of 26, James St, Bolton.

MONTGOMERY, Able Seaman, JOSEPH ROBERT. Age 23. Son of Arthur and Sarah Montgomery, of 4, Hertford Square, Butts, Coventry.

NOLAN, Petty Officer, PATRICK.

RICKETTS, Stoker 1st Class, HENRY LEONARD. Age 24. Son of Henry Ricketts, of 2, Beaconfield Rd, Willesden Green, London. Husband of Dorcas Elizabeth Ricketts, of 23, Brandon Rd, Laira, Plymouth.

WHITE, Able Seaman, ALFRED. Age 23. Son of Annie T. White, of Higher Terrace, Harrowbarrow, St Dominick, Cornwall.

PORTSMOUTH NAVAL MEMORIAL

BLACKMAN, Stoker 1st Class, JAMES.

COOLEY, Petty Officer, WILLIAM CLARK.

FINCH, Leading Seaman, WILLIAM.

GILL, Leading Seaman, ROBERT. Husband of Eliza Mary Saker (formerly Gill), of 88, Samuel Rd, Kingston, Portsmouth.

JONES, Stoker 1st Class, EDWARD. Age 23. Son of Thomas and Grace Jones, of Dingle, Brynmawr, Llanymynech, Mont.

LORD, Ordinary Telegraphist, FREDERICK EDWIN. Age 18. Son of John Berrie Lord and Eliza Lord, of 42, Larden Rd, Acton Vale, London.

MYOTT, Engine Room Artificer 3rd Class, DOMINICK. Age 29. Son of Patrick and Mary Myott, of 23, Roches Row, Queenstown, Co. Cork.

SAVAGE, Officer's Steward 2nd Class, CHARLES HENRY. Age 26. Son of William and Ellen Mary Savage, of 66, High St, Gosport.

SAVAGE, Petty Officer Stoker, CHARLES KETTERIDGE. Age 30. Husband of Lilian Taylor (formerly Savage), of 10, Ward Rd, Eastney, Portsmouth.

TILLEY, Leading Stoker, EDMUND. Age 28. Son of James Tilley, of Coolham, Shipley, Sussex.

WHEBLE, Able Seaman, HENRY HAVELOCK. Age 30. Son of John Edward and H. Wheble, of 36, Amersham Vale, New Cross, London.

HM Submarine K-14
(2 Men)

DUNDEE EASTERN NECROPOLIS

SCOTT[3], Leading Seaman, ALEXANDER. Age 29. Husband of Elizabeth Scott, of 36, Victoria St, Dundee. Born at Aberdeen. Grave Ref. MM. 5. 379

THE ROYAL NAVY SUBMARINE MUSEUM, GOSPORT

BOWELL, Able Seaman, A.W.

Notes

1. However, no reference is made here to the two men from *K-14*.
2. The memorial, which is enclosed in two doors, is embellished with a brass plate that reads, 'Made with timber from the old *Britannia*'. This was the second training ship of the Royal Naval College at Dartmouth. Originally launched in 1869 as *Prince of Wales*, she was renamed *Britannia* to replace an earlier ship of the same name, and in the 1890s she was a training hulk. Cdr Stocks and his peers lived in *Britannia* when under training as cadets. The Royal Naval College moved ashore and into its purpose-built accommodation in 1905. The ship was broken up in 1916, and no doubt Mrs Stocks obtained some of her timbers.
3. Leading Seaman Scott is the only man to have a named grave. He appears to have been one of the only two Scotsmen among the casualties.

Bibliography and Sources

Allan, James, *Isle of May*, Tervor Ltd, 2000
Barry, Rev. John, *Naval battles that never were*, 1990
Brown, D.K., *Before the Ironclad*, Conway Maritime Press, 1990
Coles, Alan, *Three before breakfast*, Kenneth Mason, 1979
Evans, A.S., *Beneath the Waves*, 1986
Harris, John, *Lost at Sea*, Guild Publishing, 1990
Hendrie, William F., *The Forth at War*, Birlinn Ltd, 2002
Humble, Richard, *Before the Dreadnought*
Ranft, B. McL., *The Beatty Papers. Vol. 1. 1902–1918*, Scolar Press for the Navy Records Society, 1989
Regan, Geoffrey, *Naval Blunders*, André Deutsch Ltd, 2001
Tall, J.J. and Kemp, Paul, *HM Submarines in Camera*, Sutton Publishing, 1996
The Naval Review 1919 (with acknowledgement to Lt H.M. Fardell RN)
White, Colin, *The Heyday of Steam*, Kenneth Mason, 1983
Wikipedia, the online encyclopedia

Commonwealth War Graves Commission
Leir family genealogical website
Royal Navy Historical Branch, Ministry of Defence
Royal Navy Museum, Portsmouth, Hampshire
Submarine Museum, Gosport, Hampshire
The National Archives, Kew, Surrey
The Times of London

Index

Page numbers in *italics* refer to illustrations.